THROUGH THESE
Doors

THROUGH THESE

A MUSTARD SEED FAITH

Theresa A. Harris-Tigg, PhD

THROUGH THESE DOORS
A MUSTARD SEED FAITH

iUniverse books may be ordered through booksellers or by contacting:

iUniverse
1663 Liberty Drive
Bloomington, IN 47403
www.iuniverse.com
844-349-9409

Because of the dynamic nature of the internet, any web addresses or links contained in this book may have changed since publication and may no longer be valid. The views expressed in this work are solely those of the author and do not necessarily reflect the views of the publisher, and the publisher hereby disclaims any responsibility for them.

Any people depicted in stock imagery provided by Getty Images are models, and such images are being used for illustrative purposes only. Certain stock imagery © Getty Images.

ISBN: 978-1-6632-3255-7 (sc)
ISBN: 978-1-6632-3289-2 (hc)
ISBN: 978-1-6632-3256-4 (e)

Library of Congress Control Number: 2021924872

Print information available on the last page.

iUniverse rev. date: 02/16/2022

To my grandchildren: Xaiver, Arius, Jaylen, Armon, Jasmin, Brooklyn, Javon, Izeal IV, Dante, Jason, Jayden; and great-grandchildren: Jayliyah, King Ezra, Jaylen (JuJu); and precious great-grandbabies on the way

In memory of Matthew N. Harris, Dorothy L. Harris, Earline Tolan, Dolores Whitt, and Robert C. Fugate

In honor of my husband Robert and children: Marvin, Ebony, and Jason

Dr. Theresa Harris-Tigg is a compassionate lady with a prayer on her lips, a smile on her face and a hug in her arms. Her excitement and love of life and family, joy in the teachings of the Lord, inspires our New Covenant UCC congregation to keep looking forward with hope and peace. We are so blessed that Theresa is sharing her life with us.

I am a retired educator and self-published author of four books. My first book was a personal Chapbook of poetry called "Back in the Day." Several memoirs published later, then my last one, a book of short stories, "Whisperers of Secrets," published in 2019.

Peace, Priscilla Y. Hill

CONTENTS

INTRODUCTION

As a teenager, I always believed that I had angels watching over me. I started to think this way when I was a small child being reared in the church. In our home, we had house rules. If we did not get up and go to church on Sunday, we were not allowed to go to the movies or hang out with our friends. As a young person, going to church every Sunday was difficult at first. However, I was encouraged to read the Bible, and I learned a lot about faith. Hebrews 11:1 declares, "Now faith is confidence in what we hope for and assurance about what we do not see." From my childhood home to the very recent announcement of precious great-grandbabies on the way, each of these moments have shaped the course of my faith. I have had many experiences in my lifetime. Some events I knew would change my life, while with others I didn't realize the impact until years later. In retrospect, I realize that I had a mustard seed kind of faith as a child, grown to a full, mountain-moving faith as an adult. All my experiences played a role and need to be shared.

> "Jesus replied, '…truly I tell you, if you have faith as small as a mustard seed, you can say to this mountain, 'move from here to there, and it will move. Nothing will be impossible for you.'" Matthew 17:20–21a

ONE

The Beginning

When I was a little girl, I remember jumping out of bed and running out of my bedroom to instantly open the big wooden sliding doors in my parents' apartment. I would first wait at the door, pass my hands over my hair and face quickly, straighten my nightgown, and with my heart pounding in my chest, I would declare my rise out of my sleep. The first thing on my mind every morning was to be the first person through those doors. This ritual marked the start of a fresh new day, and I knew something wonderful would happen. Mama would laugh unrestrainedly at my morning ritual and play acting, because she really liked those doors as well. She would stroll to those big, beautiful, thick brown doors in such an expressive way that would convey something, that would grab my dad's attention. Her long white nightgown would sway rhythmically from side to side, back and forth as she walked all the way through those doors. She had an air about her walk that signified that she was assured of her husband's love.

I would always let Mama know how much I liked the way she walked through those doors. "Mama! That is how I want to walk when I grow up; just like you. Show me how to do that, Mama!"

Mama would instantly quiet my passionate yearnings to walk like her, to be like her. She would quickly affirm my unique and original play as the absolute best. She would ask me how I felt as I walked through the doors. I would tell her that I felt important and that it felt good. She would respond by telling me to keep being myself in all I do.

As a child, I loved to hear my mom say my nickname. She'd put such emphasis on this humorous short version of my real name. "Resa" was short for Theresa. My older sister, Dolores, had two friends, one named Theresa and another Gwendolyn, and that is primarily how my sister Gwen and I got our names. However, the nickname "Resa" was distinct, and I was never told its origin.

My mom was such a beautiful woman. She was about four feet eleven with a round, chestnut brown face and big puffy cheeks. Her skin was flawless, with tiny brown freckles on each cheek. She always wore reddish lipstick and absolutely loved red on her lips. Her bosom was well endowed, and she wore good bras that showed off her beautiful gifts. Mom had strong, curved legs. She walked with confidence in her heels, and Mama loved to wear heels. They were not stilettos, just plain two to two-and-a-half-inch pumps. She would say it is part of a real woman's wardrobe. I don't think I ever saw my mother in flat shoes or sneakers. She wore slippers or what we called house shoes around the kitchen and perhaps out to the yard.

We lived in a huge apartment with a neon-sign business below us. Our living room was spacious and open, and the room was filled with plastic-covered couches and armchairs, a coffee table, two end tables, and off-white lamps. The area was great for children. We had plenty of space to run around inside and play with our riding toys. My parents loved to entertain friends and family at the house. They did not have parties, but they had friends over to discuss politics, church, or to play cards. My dad loved to play a card game called "bid whist," and my mom preferred to play two card games called "pitty-pat" and "tunk." I enjoyed watching my parents with their friends, and my dad could hold his own very well in conversations and at playing cards.

This huge apartment house was located at 588 Broadway Street on the corner of Monroe Street in Buffalo, New York. There were two floors of living space in this building. I loved living on Broadway Street. It extends from downtown Buffalo, through the city and into a suburban area named Lancaster, New York. The downtown location was a prominent one, designated by city officials for parades and official processions honoring a particular occasion or person visiting the city of Buffalo. Because we lived on the corner of Broadway and Monroe, we always had front row seats in the very important person (VIP) section of the pavement. We would run right out the front door, and Mama and Daddy would allow us to sit on the sidewalk curb to watch the parade move down the street. Long after our family moved from Broadway and Monroe Streets, we would return to that corner to be a part of the festivities. Once, when I was about eight years old, I was sitting with my family at the corner watching the procession go down Broadway Street, and I noticed that all the grown-ups seemed to be aware and anxious about something or someone in the motorcade. The adults were standing, cheering, and guessing who might be in the parade. You would have thought it was Jesus, as they were very excited and hopeful about being able to see one big expensive car that was driving down the street. I found out later that the occupants of the car were President John F. Kennedy and his wife, Jacqueline Kennedy Onassis.

Around the time I was five years old, my parents purchased their first home at 62 Timon Street, between Best and High Streets, in Buffalo. They were gratified to be first-time homeowners. The house was a two-family house. We lived downstairs, and Dad rented out the upstairs. The floor plan was designed with the living room in the front of the house and the kitchen in the back of the house. There was a big living room, small TV room, large dining room, and medium-sized kitchen in the rear. We had lots of room for family dinners and holiday celebrations. There were four bedrooms with one bathroom. I don't know how we did it with seven family members, but I don't recall any fights over bathroom time. It was a cozy and comfortable home. There was also a full, unfinished basement.

At the time, Timon Street was a beautiful, tree-lined residential neighborhood free from business and shopping traffic. This residential area was filled with many beautiful, large, two-story homes with garages and large backyards. My parents believed this part of the city would be a good neighborhood to raise a family.

My dad worked very hard to support his family and valued the stereotypical role of the male as the prominent provider. He was not very tall in stature, maybe six feet or so. However, Dad was very tall in character. He had a prophetic vision for my future. I was very skinny as a child, and my dad would tell me my legs looked like pencils. He then determined that I would be a teacher someday. My father's complexion was light-skinned and became darker as he aged. I always saw my parents as a sharp-looking couple.

At the time of purchase of the family home, he worked at Union Carbide, a plant located in the Western New York area. I believed he worked at the Niagara Falls location. Dad was what I called a "masculine kind of man." He was comfortable in his skin and had an undeniable clear image of how he would provide for the well-being of his family. He was raised on a farm, in a small agricultural community called Skippers, in Greensville County near Emporia, Virginia. My dad was born on February 23, 1922, to Fedolia and Etta Harris and was one of twelve children. At one point, when almost grown, he chose to release himself from the daily chores on the farm. Dad dreamed about moving North and making a life for himself. He left the rural area of Skippers and his siblings to start his own autonomous life.

Daddy met Mama in Hampton, Virginia, and told me that he knew from the very beginning of their relationship that she would become his wife. Even though Mom worked, she would make sure dinner was ready for Daddy when he came home from work. Mama was born a little less than one hundred miles away from Skippers in Hampton, Virginia, on July 21, 1927. After completing a laborious day's work at the plant, Daddy had a ritual he would carry out most evenings. He would wash up, eat dinner, and then watch cowboy TV shows until he fell asleep. Especially on weekends, I remember sitting on the floor in front of him watching *Gunsmoke*, with Marshall Matt Dillon. This was his routine until he started working and fixing up houses as a side hustle. He assembled a group of friends who worked on rehabilitating their own properties and those of others. This group of men were like-minded, industrious men who became great friends. My dad's longstanding colleague and friend was T. C. Oftentimes, I would call him Uncle T. C.

During my childhood years, I noticed Mom and Dad were very playful and flirtatious with each other. I can remember the gentle hugs and whispering going on between them on Saturday mornings. It made me feel good to watch them. Dad took the role of provider very seriously, so my mother did not work because of a necessity to help with the financial management of bills. Momma valued a woman having her own money in her pocketbook. I would find myself watching the interactions between my dad and mom constantly. My mom certainly had Dad's instinctive attention. His eyes would wander all around her body, up and down. If she thought anyone else noticed their playing and flirting, she would quickly bat his hands away and playfully say, "Stop it, Nat! Leave me alone now." However, it was clear to me that she enjoyed this attention. As a child, it was aspirational for my future relationships.

Daddy was secure regarding Mama's mantra that a woman must always have her own money to do with what she pleases. She did not like the idea of having to ask for money from her husband. It did not matter to my father either way; it was a source of pride for him to be the sole provider for his family. Dad never forgot about his siblings and other family members in Skippers. My aunt Pauline, one of dad's sisters, told me that when she was a child, Dad always told her that he would always look after her and not leave her. Aunt Pauline said she was so disappointed when my dad left Skippers to be on his own. Eventually, many of Daddy's brothers and sisters came north to Buffalo to start their lives outside of the agriculture and farming lifestyles. Some of Dad's family members lived with us until they were able to provide for themselves.

Daddy looked good in his church suits and anytime he went out of the house for church-related affairs. He served in his church often as a handyman and sexton. He was self-taught in the areas of carpentry and plumbing. He believed solidly in stereotypical gender roles, assigning jobs based on gender for his children until we left our parents' home to be on our own. Boys clearly had to do the manual, laborious tasks around the house. Boys were compelled to mop the kitchen floor, take out the garbage, and maintain a clean and trash-free driveway and yard outside of the house. Their seasonal work involved cutting the grass and shoveling snow. Girls were expected to do some basic cooking, setting the table for dinner, light house cleaning, and keeping the interior of the house straightened up and aesthetically pleasing. Around the time my oldest sister married and left home, I was strongly encouraged to learn how to manage a house financially. My dad explained to me how to read insurance policies, pay utility bills, mortgage statements, and tax bills, and how to put money away for savings. He echoed my mother's opinion about women having their own money. He would tell me that young ladies should know where the household money is going every week. I enjoyed learning from my dad. I believed his money management guidance was sowing seeds of preparation for something later in my life.

Very often, we would return to the old neighborhood on Broadway Street. The area evolved into multiple commercial and residential properties. A very famous local department store called Sattler's at 998 Broadway Street was the place to go. On any given day, my parents would run into friends, church members, or neighbors there shopping. The store sold clothes for the entire family. It also sold food and fruitcakes. Down the street, there was Liberty Shoes, where we purchased shoes and sneakers for the whole family. Norben's was another store my mom loved to frequent, located on Fillmore Ave. The store sold clothes also. I think the clothes at Norben's were more reasonably priced than at Sattler's. I remember Mama would take us there, and we would run all around the store. Mama would plead for us to stop being troublesome. She had to plead frequently, because four of her five children were with her most of the times. The four younger siblings were defined as stair steps because we were very close in age. Norben's stands out in my memory because many times Mama did not buy anything while shopping there. However, I did notice that Mama would meet friends there who seemed to be at the store as often as we were.

When we moved to Timon Street in 1958, there were many white people who lived on this quiet residential street, but it very quickly changed to a majority African American neighborhood. I remember this old white neighbor, Mr. Shubert, who lived right next door to our house. His house was a two-family house like ours, and he had two giant statues of owls on the base of the railing on his front porch. Mr. Shubert was as strange as the owls; both seemed to keep a watchful eye on all the happenings in the neighborhood.

He would often come out the front door of his house and just stare at the black children playing in the street. He became especially acquainted with my second oldest brother, Philip. Mr. Shubert would call out his name two or three times a day. He really did not want anything; sometimes he would just ask my brother to pick up some garbage on the street. Phil did not always want to answer Mr. Shubert's call, but we were taught to be nice to everyone you meet, especially adults. Then one day Mr. Shubert was gone (or he moved off the street).

Timon Street was undeniably a community. Everybody knew everybody and their family. If you got in trouble at one end of your street, the neighbor would call your parents before you could make it home to share the incident with your parents. Likewise, if the neighbors learned of something wonderful that you did in school or in the neighborhood, we would get accolades and cheers from everyone up and down the street; the good news would spread from house to house.

Sometime during the summer of 1966, when I completed sixth grade, my parents were told that there would be a busing integration initiative, which would be implemented the following school year within the Buffalo public school system. We were told that in September 1966, busing desegregation would be the law for many students attending schools on the east side of Buffalo. These students would be bused to mostly white schools across town as a measure to integrate black and white students in schools. What was always interesting to me was that the all-white neighborhoods were segregated as well as the all-black neighborhoods. However, white students were not required to be bused to schools in all-black neighborhoods. This was a one-way statute.

The concept of busing desegregation was a hot topic at the time, and it was marketed to the parents by pledging to them that there would be a good quality school at the end of the long bus ride for their children. The good quality schools were magnet schools where students would be drawn to attend because of better programming and academic opportunities. The underlining theory was that the all-white schools were better because white children attended them and that was what made them better, and that the black children attending all-white schools would learn how to be better students watching and learning from white children.

My experience with busing desegregation was simply awful. My brother and I were going into seventh grade at the time and were required to ride a "cheese bus" to school every day versus walking to our neighborhood middle school nearby. The bus would pick us up near our house around 6:45 a.m. It was very early and very dark out! The bus would collect students from all around the neighborhood. Each student boarded the bus with visible frustration. Some students would stomp their feet and others would not even speak to their friends. They would slump down in the seats. Once we arrived at school, the teachers were indifferent and did not believe that the black students could learn. There was a lot of order and control procedures instituted every minute of the day. We could barely breathe without permission. After school, everyone on the bus promised to report this madness to their parents and convince them to allow us to attend the schools in our neighborhood, where we experienced a caring relationship with our teachers.

My brother and I, along with some other friends, boarded the yellow bus en route to our new school. I sat in the middle of the bus talking to my friends. My brother was sitting with his friends closer to the front. As we drove around the neighborhood picking up children from the streets surrounding Timon Street, something felt amiss. My stomach hurt because I was very anxious and could not eat my breakfast. After about forty-five minutes or so, I heard the bus driver announce that we would be in front of the school in about five minutes. He directed us to remain seated on the bus until he gave us permission to disembark.

The white bus driver warned us to sit up properly on the bus and talk quietly. He went over the bus rules, procedures, and consequences. The children on my bus were eleven, twelve, and thirteen years old. We believed we did not need this indoctrination. There were even warnings that if we did not adhere to the bus rules, the bus would not move until order was restored. Well, most of us did not want to attend the white school across town anyway, so we thought maybe misbehavior could be a means to an end.

The darkness was turning to light. I noticed there were a lot of adults standing and lining the streets near the new school. I was thinking that they were there to welcome the new students to the school and the neighborhood. I am sure that is what my neighbors on Timon Street would have done. Some of the nervousness began to subside a little as we drove closer to the school. Suddenly, the bus stopped, and we remained seated as the bus driver had ordered us to do.

As we approached Public School #78 on Olympic and Berwyn Avenue, the white bus driver demanded that we should close our mouths and actively listen to his commands. By that time, I was angry because everyone on the bus was talking but no one had been out of their seats or unruly. I was not in the mood for another lecture, an "I am your boss" message directing us what to do and not do. The driver continued exhorting that we listen carefully and explicitly and follow his instructions for disembarking the bus. His boisterous harsh tone grabbed everyone's attention to the point you could hear a cotton ball drop. He ordered us to walk in a single-file line off the bus, without running, to look straight ahead and walk straight ahead to the front doors of the school. He asked us not to be concerned with anything we might hear from the adults stationed on the sidewalks adjacent to the school.

The bus driver would say, "I want everyone's attention up here. Look at me! Please listen very carefully." The bus driver's tone was a tad bit frightening as he instructed us to be quiet. He went on to insist, "When I give you the signal to stand up and get off the bus, I want you to go directly

in the school. This is very important that you do just what I ask you to do."
This little white man seemed to take our arrival very seriously. I guess
because this was a very important day when little black children would now
attend a school with mostly white children. I did not want to go.

I remember skipping in front of a few of my friends in the line on
the bus to stand behind my brother. Phil and I were a year and four days
apart. I was afraid and my brother was someone I looked to for protection
very often. For the most part, my friends and I did exactly what the bus
driver demanded. I was curious about the white people on the sidewalks.
I deliberately looked at some of them standing and noticed by the look on
their red faces and finger-pointing gestures that they were very unhappy
about something. I heard the crowd shouting at us. It was so many white
adults shouting at one time that most of what they said was inaudible, but
the one declaration that I heard loud and clear was, "Go back to where you
came from! You don't belong over here!"

The bus driver continued, "I don't want you to look to the left or the
right, but straight ahead to the front door. You are not to run! You are to
walk quickly to the front door. Do not pay attention to anyone else but the
school officials."

Well, I wondered, *who else would be trying to give us directions?*

"I mean it! If someone calls for your attention by saying, 'Hey little girl
or little boy,' you are to ignore it and continue moving quickly to get inside
the school. Do you hear me?"

When he gave us directions to stand, I quickly moved closer to the front
with my brother. I was scared at this point. I mean the bus driver did his
best to be firm yet friendly, but that dichotomy made me very nervous. I
walked closely behind my brother. When we got off the bus, we did as the
bus driver demanded. There was this older white man waving us inside.
I took a quick peek at some of the people standing on the sidewalk by the
school. Many of their faces were red and they were yelling something
directed at us.

"Get out of here! Go back where you came from. You don't belong here
at our school." I was puzzled by that, "our school." I did not know people
could own schools. Once in the school, the teachers were in administration
mode. They were yelling last names out and pointing to where students
should report. There were no hellos or welcome to school for any of us. I
thought, *What in the world!* This was totally different from Public School

#39, where we were like family. There, as the days rolled by, all of us had begun to settle in and focus on our schoolwork ahead of us.

Once we moved inside the school, I experienced a short bout of relief. It was not as noisy as outside, and it appeared less terrifying. However, it was cold and chaotic. Last names were being called loudly and randomly from three or four adults at the same time, along with room numbers. We were urged to not tarry and get to our homerooms quickly. Every adult yelled directives with a heightened sense of urgency in their tone. I thought perhaps the people outside were going to come through the front door any minute to do something to us. The remainder of the day in the classrooms was pretty much like the beginning of that first day of school. We were exposed to more mandates and laws to quickly absorb and respond accordingly.

During this period in my life, my family attended a racially diverse church, which was blocks away from our house on Sherman and Sycamore Streets. The church was named Salem United Church of Christ (UCC). There we worshipped together with white and black members; our pastor at the time was a white male. My oldest sister, Dolores, had begun attending this church with her friends. She convinced our parents to visit, and shortly thereafter they became members. The entire family worshipped there until the church physically closed in 1973. It was an intergenerational church as well. There were as many children as there were adults and senior citizens. The adults were very kind and nurturing and exhibited love in all their interactions. In the summer, all the young people attended our denomination's summer camp at Dunkirk Conference Grounds in Dunkirk, New York. Salem UCC had scout troops and a coffee house where the teenagers gathered to hang out and talk about their experiences at school, church, and home.

I always felt supported by the adults at Salem UCC. I attended Sunday school regularly and confirmation classes. My spiritual foundation was born out of that congregation. The interaction was akin to our family experiences in the neighborhood on Timon Street. Salem UCC was a family and community church.

Justice and inclusiveness for all was an important part of the ministries and the doctrine of the members at this church. I remember when my parents and a group of adults from Salem UCC planned and traveled to Washington, DC, in late summer, for the March on Washington for Jobs and Freedom on August 28, 1963. My parents and other church members were the United Church of Christ delegation to the March. I cannot tell how much that pilgrimage stood out in my mind then and today. They were sowing seeds in fertile soil of walking with humility and promoting justice.

When we came home from school after our first day of the busing integration experience, I believed in my heart that our parents would hear how awful the school day was for the children in the neighborhood and would clearly be able to demand a reversal of the busing desegregation law. Our parents were powerful and conscientious people who helped others fight for their rights and freedom; surely they could demand that their children attend a neighborhood school versus attending a school where, clearly, we were not wanted. Unfortunately, and critically disappointing, they were not able to get a reversal of the school district's mandate regarding the all-white school we were required to attend.

Before the busing desegregation initiative, I attended Public School #39 (now named Martin Luther King Multicultural Institute), located at the corner of Timon and High Streets. It was a neighborhood school. All my friends went to that school. Most of the teachers were white; however, for the most part, they seemed to be caring and passionate about teaching and learning. It was also a benefit to live so close to the school. I witnessed several times teachers walking to a student's house to talk with the parents about progress or problems.

Last night, I begged Mama to fix this situation; so that I could go to the middle school closer to our house. She told me that there was nothing she could do about it because the school district had decided to begin integrating the schools, and busing was going to be the strategy to make that happen. "But you and Daddy decide what school we can go to, right? How can the school tell the parents what school their children have to attend?" My mom shrugged her shoulders and told me that they did not have a choice in this matter.

I remember one day in my English class when the white male teacher and a black male student was arguing about one of the characters in the story that we were reading. The teacher thought the character demonstrated flat characteristic, whereas the black male student saw the character as round and vibrant. The teacher was becoming increasingly angry as the student continued to talk over him and reiterate his point over and over. The teacher finally went over to where the student was seated and snatched him out of his seat. I was shocked! The black male student attempted to hold on to the teacher's shirt as he was grabbed. The teacher pushed the student against the windowsill where the window was opened and forced his head out the window. Then, suddenly the student was released from the teacher's grasp, and he stumbled back to his assigned seat. I was crying because the student was my friend and neighbor. The teacher never said another word. Then, the change of class bell loudly broke through the still and alarming atmosphere.

When I arrived home on that day, I could not wait to tell my mother. She was working at a nursing home so I had to wait to tell her. I knew for sure that my parents would see the light and do whatever they needed to do to get my brother and I out of that school. Well, my parents were very upset after hearing what happened in my English classroom. My dad shared it with the neighbors while the news was reporting the desegregation plan was "going well." He was upset because every day, when my brother and I came home, we had a different story of an inappropriate and oppressive learning environment. I was so glad my dad and mom understood our fears and anger. I was confident at that point that my brother and I would be returned to the schools in our neighborhood. My parents shared our concerns with the neighbors, and impromptu gatherings on porches and in driveways were arranged. At some point, my parents conveyed that my brother and I would have to complete the eighth grade at Public School #78. That declaration stunned me! I was outraged! It was the first time I saw my parents as powerless! The school integration plan was unsound, because the underlying belief was that little black children needed to sit next to little white children to make us better students, regardless of the racist experiences we had to endure.

My father had strict family rules while we were growing into our teenage years. He worked nights and needed to ensure that we were safe. These rules were nonnegotiable and carried stiff consequences if violated. First, we were required to be in the house by the time the streetlights came on. This meant that in the summer, we had to be in the house by 9:00 p.m. and in the winter, we had to be in by 4:30 p.m. Another rule was that we could not bring home any grades in the core academic subjects lower than 85. One year, in seventh grade, I received a 75 in math. My father was adamant, as I attempted to offer valid reasons, as to why I should not be punished for breaking the grade point rule. My reasons did not matter to him. I spent the entire summer on punishment in the house without TV and limited outside play to the backyard. It was brutal.

Another rule of thumb had to do with church attendance. My father and mother held respectable positions on boards in the church. The entire family attended nearly every Sunday. The rule was that if you did not attend church, you could not go anywhere else for the rest of that week, so if I had plans to go to the movies after school with my friends, I had to make sure I went to church the Sunday before. Going to church was not a big lift for me. I loved attending Salem United Church of Christ. There were a lot of young people my age that attended. We had very impressive Sunday school teachers. One of my teachers was Mr. Guy Outlaw. My parents told me he was the first African American male principal in Buffalo. He had a Boston accent, and I loved to hear him speak. He made the Sunday school lesson intriguing and interesting, because his accent and his cadence drew me into the Bible lessons and scriptures with delight.

By the time I graduated eighth grade and started my high school experience, I was angry. I felt betrayed by an educational system that would snatch black students from a supportive neighborhood school to attend a cold middle school where no one really cared about us or wanted us in their all-white school. At Bennett High School, I had my first black teacher. In fact, there was two black female teachers at my high school: Mrs. Henderson and Ms. Blue. I had Mrs. Henderson as my gym teacher. She was a beautiful looking woman who carried herself exquisitely. Her hair and makeup were perfectly applied. She sported shorts and sneakers as her uniform in gym class and she always behaved like a professional and thoughtful teacher. She commanded good behavior from her students. She directed us to come to class prepared and ready to participate in all gym activities. Ms. Blue was a gorgeous black woman as well. She also was a gym teacher who exuded excellence personally and professionally. I marveled at these two ladies and would deliberately watch their interactions with students and other teachers.

One day after class, Mrs. Henderson asked me the name of my middle school where I last attended. Well, she opened the floodgates because I went on to tell her about my horrible experiences at my middle school and what the teacher did to my friend because he disagreed about the attributes of a character. Mrs. Henderson shared that my anger is palpable! She told me that the best retribution is to do better than any of those teachers would expect from me. My gym teacher took time over several sessions to hear my pain and push my thinking. She asked me to consider forgiving the teacher and the angry white adults outside the school for the sake of my own well-being. I listened attentively to Mrs. Henderson, but it took some time for me to get to that place emotionally. Mrs. Henderson and Ms. Blue were a bridge over troubled waters, and I am forever grateful.

High school graduation was an expected outcome for every child in our family. Postsecondary expectations consisted of college or work. My parents required you to do one or the other. When I spoke to the high school counselors, they basically encouraged me to work versus go to college. There was no support to evaluate college courses at that time.

In the latter part of the summer after high school, I realized I was pregnant. My boyfriend at the time was a young man from the neighborhood. Donald and I had been talking and calling ourselves boyfriend–girlfriend since eighth grade, maybe longer. We saw each other every day. He was a nice guy and very attentive. He went to a vocational high school, and I went to an academic high school. It is funny now, but high school was probably the first time that Donald and I had to find time to see each other because of commitments to school, sports, and working.

I was afraid to come right out and tell my dad. He was strict about what would and would not go on in his house. My two brothers and youngest sister discussed ways to come up with a plan to tell my dad. One evening after dinner, my brother Phil gave the cue; I went into the bathroom and got under the tub. We had a beautiful bathtub with legs, and I was able to squeeze my body under that tub just in case dad wanted to act crazy. Once Phil said the words, "Dad and Mom, Resa is pregnant, and she is scared to tell you." It was silent in the kitchen. I could not hear another word. I remained in the bathroom crying quietly. My oldest brother, Nathan, began to reason with my dad about my actions by reminding him that I completed high school and was working and earning my own money.

"Where is Theresa?" my dad asked. He used my name! He was not happy about this, but he remained unusually calm. I do not remember getting spankings from our parents, but we would be remanded to our bedrooms for extended periods of time. When I finally came out of the bathroom, my dad resolutely informed me that I need to leave the house. I remember my mother was very quiet when Dad told me to leave. I thought about her silence for a long time. I did not know what to do about that fact. I wondered if I ever could get over that she did not fight for me to stay in the home. Gwen, my youngest sister, was very quiet at the time, but I knew she did not want me to be kicked out of the house. My oldest sister, Dolores, told my parents that she would not see me in the streets and took me to live with her family. I remember Lois, affectionate name for Dolores, telling her husband that she did not know how long I would be staying with them. She claimed Daddy just needed some time to calm down. She did not say anything about Mama's response, or shall I say lack of response, but it bothered me tremendously.

During the time I lived at Lois's house, she would teach me and my boyfriend how to encourage each other, save money, and prepare for having a family and running a household. She helped to plan the marriage ceremony and our household budget for the apartment. I stayed with my sister and her family several months before marrying my boyfriend in December 1972. One month later, January 28, 1973, I gave birth to our son, Marvin Adriel. I gave him the first name of my obstetrician. The delivering of my son was very painful. Marvin was a preemie. At one point during delivery, I grabbed and begged the doctor to help me because I felt like I was going to die. I told him I would name the baby after him if he would stop the pain. Of course, having one of your patients name their baby after you was no great benefit to the doctor; but it was my way of showing the doctor that he could be a blessing during this birthing experience.

Marvin was born at 3 lbs., 2 oz. after a five-month gestation period. He was diagnosed as premature. I learned later that this premature birth was directly related to my prolonged stress and smoking cigarettes. I started smoking at around age thirteen. I would sneak cigarettes from my mom's pack at night and smoke in the bathroom. I didn't smoke a lot of cigarettes in the beginning, maybe three a day. However, I quickly increased the number of cigarettes I smoked when I found out I was pregnant and again when my dad kicked me out the house. I enjoyed smoking cigarettes at first, because I liked the way my mom acted while smoking her cigarettes. Smoking seemed like a treat she would give herself at times. Later, I think I smoked because it seemed to settle my fears and worries.

By the time of the marriage ceremony, Donald had paid the security deposit on an apartment and purchased all the furniture needed for the apartment. My husband worked very hard to provide the best for us. Ironically, our first apartment was back in our old neighborhood on Timon Street. Just as it was when we were children, it remained a very supportive community. My husband and I were seen as a favorite couple. While our neighbors did not endorse sex before marriage, many of them shared their endorsement of our marriage. We were beloved young adults from the neighborhood, and our village knew our families well.

About a month after the wedding, Marvin was born. My dad had mellowed out and decided to move past my transgressions. Some would say that my dad did not like my husband. They had many arguments; but I think my dad did not like that I was a pregnant teenager and Donald was the guy. Dad and Mom calmly and reservedly attended the wedding. I wore my sister-in-law's fuchsia high school graduation dress as the "wedding gown." We were happily married couple for a very long time, and thank God for Lois, we handled our financial affairs admirably.

Dolores taught Donald and me everything she knew to set up and run a household; she started us off with a good foundation. It almost felt like she was the mother-of-the bride. I never really believed that my dad hated me or that he was angry with me for getting pregnant. I sensed his deep disappointment. My dad started teaching me to drive at age fourteen, and I got my license at the legal age of sixteen. He was proud that I was one of the first young girls on Timon Street with a license. He wanted me to be a smart, independent young lady. I was aware of how proud my dad was of the things I was able to accomplish at fourteen and fifteen years old working at supermarkets. In his eyes, I was apparently obedient and determined to do well in life. He had high hopes for my future as a teacher.

TWO
The Family

"Don't you see the children are God's best gift? The fruit of the womb his generous legacy?"

John 127:3 MSG

Donald and I had a three-bedroom apartment in the old neighborhood on Timon Street. We lived upstairs in a beautiful and large two-family house, closer to High Street. The landlord was a minister who took good care of the property. The apartment was immaculate. There was lots of beautiful original wood throughout the apartment. My neighbors on both sides of the apartment and across the street were people who literally watched my husband and I grow up from childhood, through young adulthood, from young adults to parenthood. These people were the real deal. They continued the role as supportive village family. My next-door neighbors, Rita and Curtis Mills, would share a lot of parenting advice with us. Marvin was very small, and we learned early on that he suffered petit mal seizures. Rita and Curtis prayed with us and reassured us that Marvin would grow up and do well in life.

Rita and I became very close as friends, and we would talk about everything. She really helped me to think through the overwhelming significance of being a teenage bride and mother. She knew my parents and respected them. However, she made space for me to vent in confidence and afforded me a compassionate shoulder to cry on. Rita and Curtis assisted our growth from teenagers to young parents. Almost two years later, I learned that I was pregnant with my second child. Donald and I grew up in church and knew the Lord. At this time, we were not active churchgoing members. Yet, it was at this time that we really began to get acquainted with the Lord for ourselves. We prayed for our son and our new baby on the way. We had faith that God would take care of our little family.

One evening in the middle of March 1974, on Best near Pershing Streets, a half mile from our apartment and my parents' house, a few young men stole a car. As the men traveled to the corner of Pershing at Best Street in the stolen vehicle, they T-boned my brother Phil's car. The stolen vehicle was unable to stop because the brakes were inoperable. The stolen vehicle crashed into the small Pinto with great force. Phil had come home on a break from his duty in the air force. Shortly before his arrival in Buffalo, he learned that he was going to be a dad for the first time and, at about the same time, become an uncle again. His wife Carolyn and I were both pregnant at the same time. Carolyn was having her first child, and I was having my second. We were on our way to a Chinese restaurant on Main Street when the collision happened.

Both Carolyn and I were approximately five weeks since gestation. She was sitting in the front passenger seat next to her husband, and I was sitting directly behind the driver. My husband was sitting directly behind Carolyn. Most of us suffered serious injuries. It was reported that Donald was ejected from the vehicle and was found walking down the street with a blood-covered face and confused. A friend of ours named Vinton saw him and was able to assist him getting medical attention from the paramedics. I was never told how Carolyn got out of the vehicle, but I learned she did not have any serious injuries. My brother and I had serious injuries. Both of us severed our femur (thighbone) completely. I was told that the firemen and EMT's had to utilize the "jaws of life" equipment to remove me from the entangled and crushed Pinto. I suffered a fractured wrist and bruises on my back. We were rushed by ambulance to two different hospitals. I ended up at Meyer Hospital, a county hospital that specialized in traumatic injuries. My brother and husband were taken to our neighborhood facility, Deaconess Hospital.

My mother called Phil's air force reporting station and informed the military of the car accident involving my brother and sister-in-law. The officers over my brother's unit exhibited empathy but clearly informed her that Phil would need to report to the North Dakota base as soon as medically possible. My mother was taken aback by the order. My mother was asked to provide all the essential hospital and physician information for the military's follow-through. Later, after a surgical insertion of a steel rod in his femur, Phil returned to his military duties.

Upon arrival at Meyer Hospital, I was unconscious. My sister Dolores provided identification and medical history information. She told every medical personnel she spoke with that I had just learned that I was pregnant. She pleaded with the medical professionals to be gentle with me. Dolores worked as an operating room technician at another hospital and understood procedures and practices involving trauma. Cell phones were not on the scene yet, and my sister found it very difficult to keep up with what was going on with my husband, our brother, and sister-in-law.

My dad was solemn and chauffeured my mother and Lois (both women did not drive) back and forth to the hospitals. In about ten days or so, I awoke on the orthopedic floor at Meyer Hospital. I thought I had died, because I was in a large, open room with a white woman clothed in all white. I was scared and confused. Her name was Marie. She was my roommate and assured me that I was not dead but instead in a hospital after a terrible car accident. Marie informed me that my mother and sister had been waiting at my bedside for me to wake up. I did not understand much and wanted to talk with my husband.

My mom and Lois arrived in my hospital room shortly after my awaking, and they tried to reassure me I was going to be okay. They told me that my husband was at Deaconess Hospital. Donald needed facial plastic surgery. He received lots of cuts and bruises on his face from the shattered windshield. They told me my brother was at the same hospital as my husband. Carolyn escaped any serious injuries but was pretty shaken up. My head was swirling trying to keep up with all the updates on everyone. It felt like being on an amusement ride where you have no control of what is happening. I became nauseated and dizzy and vomited all over my bed.

I was trying to gain a sense of self-control and remembered that I was pregnant. "Mom, how is my baby?" My sister's eyes dropped from view and her face suddenly looked very sad. I looked around the room for my mom and her whole body was turned away from me. My heart started banging severely in my chest. It was pounding in my ear, and I was terrified it was going to come through my chest. Sweat started to pour down my face and breathing was tough. As I started to sit up, I noted that I was constrained in some way. The pain hit me like a ton of bricks. My left leg began throbbing terribly. I thought, *Jesus, help me, because I am dying!*

The dreadful news about my baby was incomprehensible. Lois sat on the bed and informed me that the doctors at the hospital do not think you are pregnant anymore. A nurse came in the room and reported that I lost a lot of blood. Because I was very early in the pregnancy, it is highly likely that the pregnancy was terminated. The nurse just blurted those words out very matter of fact. Now my sister was always the family go-to-person for medical clarification and understanding. I questioned how they would know for sure I lost my baby because I lost a lot of blood. I remember screaming, "Why?" and saying, "I lost my baby!" over and over. I just could not believe it. Later that day, I could not say anything else about my pregnancy. I did not have the strength. My heart continued pounding in my chest. The nurse left the room while my sister and mom and I sat silently in my denial.

Early the next morning, another doctor came to see me. She called my marital name to wake me up. She told me she was a resident obstetrician on call, and it was clear to her that my pregnancy was terminated due to the loss of large volumes of blood. She reiterated that I was very early in the pregnancy and the survival rate for an early-term embryo involved with the critical loss of a large volume of blood is very low. At that point, a weird feeling came over me. I could see her mouth move; but I could not hear what she was saying. I felt dizzy. I was going to pass out trying to focus and listen. Then, a surgical procedure called a D&C as soon as possible was declared necessary. She needed me to sign and consent to this procedure. I felt like I was submerged underwater, with every sound muffled. I could know her trying-to-be kind face was advising me to allow her to do something to me. I called on the Lord, surrendered to this woozy feeling, and went back to sleep.

Dolores was adamant and did not want me to have the D&C procedure. She stated that I needed to be stronger physically. She reminded my mother that another doctor brought this procedure up last week while I was unconscious. My sister demanded at that time the procedure be postponed until I was awake. When my sister and I talked privately, I agreed that I would not have this procedure until I felt stronger. In addition to trying to make sense out of losing a baby and having a surgical procedure, I was trying to negotiate my darn hospital bed to which my left leg was forcibly constrained by a bungie cord and three bars of weights. I learned that my thighbone was completely severed in half, a complete break. Because I was pregnant upon arrival to the emergency room, the orthopedic technique with the weights was determined to be most effective to begin the process of healing for my broken thighbone. My brother, having the same injury to his thigh, had already received a metal rod inserted in his thigh during surgery. The surgical intervention was not an option for me. It looked like a pulley system. It was not comfortable, and it caused me to be imprisoned literally and spiritually. All I could do was scream in horror.

Shortly thereafter, I found myself on the psychiatric ward. The doctors advised I needed psychiatric and mental support for my denial and lack of acceptance of the aborted pregnancy, and they were right! I needed help, but I would not get what I needed from them. I prayed and prayed and asked God to help me understand what happened to my baby. I believed I was still pregnant. I began to proclaim that fact every day. I refused to entertain any discussion of having a surgical procedure to scrape my uterus and thus kill my baby. By this time, Lois began sharing my situation with some of the doctors she worked with in surgery. She sought out a highly reputable orthopedic surgeon who would look at my condition and provide best practice options for how I should proceed with the issue of my femur. Dr. Cole was phenomenal. He listened to me with compassion. He discussed my surgical options to unbind me from my hospital bed. The surgical insertion of a metal rod was an option if, in fact, the pregnancy was terminated. If the pregnancy is still viable, the surgical option would not be advised and the weights would remain on my leg in place in the hospital bed for about three to four months to allow my thigh to fuse together evenly and completely. This meant that I would have to remain in the hospital the entire time!

Finally, I told the orthopedic surgeon that I guess I am going to be here a while because I am still pregnant. There had been a lot of x-rays already taken of my femur, my back and my right arm and wrist. I demanded that they shield my stomach and pelvic area so that I did not receive x-rays seeping into my uterus. Dr. Cole accepted my perspective at that point. I think I really convinced him that the possibility of my being pregnant was just as real as the medical prognosis that the pregnancy was terminated. He also encouraged me from an aesthetic point. He said I will make out better because I will not have a long surgical scar running down my leg due to the insertion of a metal rod. He agreed he would continue to be the lead orthopedic doctor on my case and we would get through this together. Dr. Cole had me transferred out of the psychiatric unit and back to a regular orthopedic floor for my care. I guessed everyone would have to just wait and see! I was bound to the hospital bed for approximately four long months and happily pregnant all the while!

When I was released from the hospital in late June 1974, I had to wear a cast with a knee brace for a couple of months and undergo many more cast adjustments and changes. I delivered my beautiful daughter on September 12, 1974. God is better than good! God increased my faith in great measure. Personnel and staff from the Meyer Hospital sent beautiful gifts to my home for my baby girl. She was perfect. By the way, she was my biggest baby at birth. I guess she was in the oven a long time gaining weight and browning. Donald and I named her Ebony Efaye'. My parents were so happy and relieved. Yet Dad expressed great concern that the baby's name was Ebony; the color black. He asserted that everyone could see that she is a beautiful black baby. He could not understand why we would give her the name of the color black. My husband and I loved the name Ebony because we loved the song, "Ebony Eyes," by Rick James and Smokey Robinson. The name Efaye' came from the middle name of Donald's cousin Darlene (Doll).

Three years after that, my last child came into this world happy and healthy. He was a little boy we named Jason Donald. Jason was born on December 6, 1977. What was exciting about the birth of Jason was that we were blessed to share this precious time with my very good friend Carla Lynn. We met at Salem UCC as children and have been best friends forever. We were at the hospital during the same time, and she gave birth to a little boy named Jamar. Jason and Jamar were born a day a part and remain very good friends today. Jason's siblings were not necessarily enthusiastic about his arrival. In fact, one afternoon, Marvin and Ebony placed my baby inside their toy box to hide him from his parents. They did not want to share their parents with this new little boy.

Just before the birth of my third child, I attended Bryant & Stratton Business Institute and earned a diploma in medical office practices. I was very happy with my family but knew I did not want any more children. Three children and a husband to manage was a lot at age twenty-two. It was also evident that the picture-perfect seam in our marriage was beginning to pull apart. I did not realize that my husband was not getting the kind of attention he needed from me while, at the same time, three children left me exhausted most of the time. My oldest son's petit mal seizures were more visible and seemingly problematic. I did not really know where to put that medical situation, because Marvin was a vibrant and playful little boy. My son's pediatrician referred me to a neurologist. I knew how grand mal seizures looked, because one of my colleagues would fall out and her body would shake violently from time to time. The office staff was told to just let her be and make sure she did not hurt herself. Marvin did not have that kind of experience. He would have episodes where he would stop talking, blink, and stare for about ten seconds and then resume whatever he was saying or doing previously. Sometimes, he would forget what he was talking about. At first, his sister and brother would laugh at him, and he would laugh too. Later, as they all were growing, his siblings became worried for him, and he would remind them that they all used to laugh at his seizures. He did not want them to worry about him. He encouraged their loving banter. The neurologist confirmed that Marvin indeed had petit mal seizures. He recommended medication and monitoring to see if it remains at the level it presented or if it would get worse. Well, it never got any worse. Praise God! My oldest son, went on to play little league football and basketball and high school basketball, get married, have two children, complete a twenty-three-year term in the U.S. Army, and retire with the title, staff sergeant. Marvin is an amazing man.

Life did not get any easier at home. My husband and I seemed to always be on the edge of frustration. In 1980, we divorced, and I decided to leave our home with the children. It was a very difficult decision to leave my husband. I knew the Lord did not approve of divorce, but the relationship was eroding, and our frustrations began to increase. I think we were frustrated with each other because home was filled with a lot of stressors. My lawyer urged me to stay in the marriage a couple more years to be eligible for portions of my husband's Social Security allocation. I was twenty-six years old and just wanted to experience peace in my home. My husband was a good man, and I believed his love for his children was forever.

Shortly after Jason was born, my mother was diagnosed with kidney cancer. She noticed blood in her urine but thought it would go away on its own. Chemotherapy and radiation were recommended for her stage and level. My mother refused the chemotherapy but did some radiation. I was heartbroken when she refused chemotherapy because the doctor's prognosis was very poor without it. My mom believed chemotherapy would cause her to be sick more often, she would lose her hair, and make the quality of her life worse than the cancer could do alone. My dad was beyond bewildered learning of my mother's prognosis. He depended on my mother emotionally more then he wanted people to know. My mother, however, expressed mountain-moving faith of a strength I had not recognized anywhere before. She was clear that God had already been good to her and done great things. She would go on to handle this aggressive disease with great faith and determination. My mom's nephrologist, kidney doctor, concluded that without chemotherapy my mom would live approximately another nine to eighteen months. My mother lived two-and-a-half years after that prognosis without having any chemotherapy and with a huge dose of profound faith in the promises of God.

My mother was named Dorothy Lee Harris. Her maiden name was Goins, but she also took on the name Tolan from her stepfather. Her family and close friends called her Dot-Lee. She was the oldest in her family, with two siblings. My grandparents, Denson and Earline, were very proud of my mother and my dad and what they accomplished as a family. My grandparents loved their five grandchildren. We visited them in Washington, DC, most summers. My mother had one brother and one sister. She loved her parents and her siblings deeply. Mom had one beloved nephew, James Ray, and he always had a big place in her heart. My mother was born and raised in Hampton, Virginia. She met my dad sometime before she was eighteen years old. My dad was five years older than my mother. He persuaded my grandparents to allow him to marry my mother. He brought her to Buffalo to begin their life up North. My father was a good provider. We always had a roof over our heads, never worried if we were going to eat, and always had the things we needed. Now, my dad was not a big spender at all. We had what we needed. My mom was a lot of fun. She loved to sing and dance around the house. After church on Sundays, all of us would get a fake microphone or a broom and sing and dance. My mother also enjoyed playing cards for small amounts of money. She played with a group of friends and relatives on a regular basis.

My dad did not play cards for money. Often he would hang around my mom and her friends to enjoy the food and drinks. Many times his drinking would contribute to his talking a lot to the women there, which was a distraction for my mom. Both parents seem to be quite weary of each other. After hanging out playing cards and drinking, often arguments would ensue once they were back at home. This went on for many years. My dad knew he had a good partner, and my mom knew she had a good provider, but alcohol and gambling are strange bedfellows in a marriage.

However, it was clear to everyone that neither of them was going anywhere away from the marriage.

My mom died three days after her birthday in 1981 from right kidney cancer with metastasis to her bones. She was very young, early fifties. I was twenty-six years old, and I felt like a two-year-old child who still needed her mother. One day while Mama was in the hospital, she decided she wanted to go home. I contacted Rev. Smith, my former pastor, who ministered to and prayed with my mother often throughout her life with cancer. I thanked God for him because he was a great listener and permitted mom to share her feelings and wishes. My mom was a very loving person. She always greeted people with a smile. My dad's siblings lived near us, and they too had a special relationship with my mom.

During this difficult time in my mom's life, I was grateful that she and I were able to spend quality time together. I shared with her the challenges I faced in my marriage. She understood my decision. However, she was disappointed because she cared for my first husband. She was also concerned regarding the pressures single mothers might have raising children alone. I was not worried at all about raising my children alone. I was worried about losing my mother. I did not want to let her go. At twenty-six, I was starting to connect with her from a woman's perspective versus a young adult. I wanted to talk with her about the time Daddy kicked me out of the house and why she didn't say anything. I had so much I wanted to share with her about my future and my children.

My dad was acting in a different way during this time. He seemed to be angry that mom was dying and went in and out of depression. Some days, he would just be so frustrated that he was not helpful with the care of my mother. He would be so distant that he would not respond to requests to pick up medicine or other items my mother needed. It became clear that he was not able to care for my mom alone. Consequently, my siblings and I created a schedule where each of us would spend time taking care of mama.

The last few days of mama's life were very tough. At the time, I worked for a cardiologist, and he was generous and compassionate regarding my time out of work. This was before employee family leave plans were established. He afforded me the time I needed from work to be with my mom. During the final hours, I became so overwhelmed and anxious about her transition period. All I could think to do was lie down on the twin bed next to her. I pleaded with God to not allow my mom to suffer anymore. I wanted him to take her away peacefully and quietly. I fell asleep, and someone abruptly woke me up to inform me that mom had gone on to glory. My heart literally shattered in my chest.

Some of my siblings went with Dad to the Lewis funeral home to pick out the casket and take care of the funeral arrangements. My dad seemed to be matter-of-fact with the funeral arrangements. My parents had prepared for the time when one of them would no longer be here on earth. I am sure my dad thought he would go first. At this point, our family was attending New Covenant United Church of Christ under the pastorate of Rev. Will J. Brown. My parents were tithers and held leadership positions at the church. At the time, I requested Rev. Smith to do my mom's eulogy. My dad honored that request.

My mom had a wonderful soul, and I don't think she ever met a stranger. She was kind to everyone. During the last few weeks of my mother's life, I recall there were a few conversations with various members of the family about Mom having something to tell me. I think my mom tried to say something on many occasions, but there were so many words of guidance she wanted to give me regarding my kids. She would tell me from time to time that there is something she needs to share with me. I thought she wanted to talk about why she was silent when dad asked me to leave the house. However, I didn't want to talk about that anymore. I did not want my mother to leave me. I had forgiven her and did not want to rehash the incident again, so whatever it was that she needed to tell me never came out. It seemed very important, and she implied some members of the family knew about what she wanted to tell me. I had no clue and never thought about it again.

The funeral service was beautiful. Many people had wonderful things to say about how my mother touched their lives. The total number of people that attended the service was a living testament to her reach, in one way or the other. I remember having mixed emotions: proud and happy at one point and deeply sad the next minute. As we were preparing to go to the cemetery, several people reached out to hug me, to offer condolences, words of encouragement, and prayers. It was overwhelming and smothering. At one point, my breathing was labored, and I was gasping for air. I needed to get in the funeral car to sit before the vehicle procession to the gravesite. People meant well, but it was hard to stand still, in terrific pain. I pushed toward the funeral car when a big light-skinned man approached me to seemingly offer his condolences. I excused myself gently and told the man I needed to go and sit down. He continued to talk and move alongside of me. He told me that my mom was a beautiful person, and he will miss her tremendously. He called her Dorothy. Just the way that he said her name caused me to hold my breath. He asked if we could talk later in the week. I did not know this man from a can of paint. I thanked him for his kind words and walked with a little umph in step to the car. It was strange. I could not imagine why I should talk with this man. This solemn-looking man continued talking apprehensively as he strolled behind me. He announced he needed to tell me something and that it is not fair anymore to keep this thing not expressed aloud, since she is gone. All I could see was his mouth moving but I was incapable of hearing any more words. I was not trying to be rude, but then, I did not have the emotional strength to pay attention to a stranger going on and on. I remember him declaring that he did not want to do this, but insisting I needed to know. He promised my mother he would never say anything. But since "Dorothy" was gone, it was no longer fair to him. He asserted that he was my father. I told this man to move away from the car door and get away from me.

The ride to St. Matthew's Cemetery was long and surreal. The uncontrollable tears ran down my face like a stream of gushing water. I struggled to listen as my siblings talked about the funeral service and people who they had not seen in a long time. It seemed unbelievable that we were burying our mother at age fifty-four. I did not know where to lay my anger. Within minutes, I remembered her beauty and how much I liked being around her. I wanted the funeral car to stop moving toward the cemetery. I had not really processed her death and was not ready to see her buried in the ground. I needed my mama to help me through this very moment.

When we returned to my parents' house after the repast, I collapsed on the twin bed again. I felt defeated, like my whole life would never be good again. I remember thinking that my youngest son, Jason, was only three years old, and he would never get to know his grandmother. My children would never get to sing with the broom for the microphone and dance with their grandmother in the living room. My mother was the glue for the family. Sometimes Dad, especially when he was drinking, was distant and not connected with the family. In fact, sometimes he did not even want to be bothered with his grandchildren. You never knew what kind of mood you would find him displaying. He was cold and alone. He told me that mom was his responsibility and that we, their children, overstepped the boundaries of care with our mother. He was unwilling to admit that on occasion he was emotionally and physically unable to render care to his wife. A marriage weathering thirty-five years is more than survival; it is sacred. I did my best to keep him informed, ask for his guidance, and, when his help was slow coming or absent, to assist with the best care for my mom. I think he understood that.

Divorced with three young children, I was determined to be a good parent. Rev. Smith had a ministerial collaborator who was starting a parenting group for young single mothers at Our Savior Lutheran Church. I was not sure I needed to do that, but I promised to attend a couple of sessions. I also think my mother had something to do with this information being shared with me. I believed my mother wanted to show her support with the challenges of a single mother. I thank God, often and still, for the quiet and thoughtful ways God provided empowering guidance to me through my mother.

At the parenting classes, I met three young women who would become my very best friends for life. Debbie, Sharon, Linda, and I were raising children without the dads in the homes. The class was facilitated by Pastor Wilson of Our Savior Lutheran Church. He was a funny white man who had a talent for dry humor to help ease the stress and challenges of single parenting. Our friendship grew quickly and deeply. We assigned ourselves the second mommas to each other's children. We laughed about the funny things our children did, cried over life's disappointments, and frequently shared childrearing stories. We sought support and validation from each other. Chronologically, I am the baby in the group. Debbie and I graduated from the same high school. Linda and I worked together at a commercial insurance company. Sharon and I started our relationship at the parenting class. This age-related fact ended up being a running joke between us. We raised our children together. We attended birthdays, graduations, and weddings among our children. Later, when our children were high school age, they described our friendship like a gang because all our children could expect to hear from each of the mothers if they got out of line. The gang description became our children's forever running joke. Yet, all the children benefitted hugely from the collective love of this gang.

We are single parent survivors. While raising our children, we found time for relaxation and entertainment. We would occasionally go out to a concert or to a local bar where we knew the owners and patrons well. We danced and listened to music. We had a good time. We sought more job-site trainings as well as pursued continuing education credits. We raised our children in church and nurtured their own faith through attendance at confirmation classes and participating in worship service as acolytes. And yes, we had romantic suitors and pursuits. There are so many stories I could talk about with regards to the budding relationships with the different guys we met, but that truly is a book of its own.

THREE

"Wait for Love"

"LOVE NEVER GIVES UP. LOVE CARES MORE FOR OTHERS THAN FOR SELF. LOVE
DOESN'T WANT WHAT IT DOESN'T HAVE. LOVE DOESN'T STRUT, DOESN'T HAVE A
SWELLED HEAD, DOESN'T FORCE ITSELF ON OTHERS, ISN'T ALWAYS "ME FIRST,"
DOESN'T FLY OFF THE HANDLE, DOESN'T KEEP SCORE OF THE SINS OF OTHERS,
DOESN'T REVEL WHEN OTHERS GROVEL, TAKES PLEASURE IN THE FLOWERING
OF TRUTH, PUTS UP WITH ANYTHING, TRUSTS GOD ALWAYS, ALWAYS LOOKS
FOR THE BEST, NEVER LOOKS BACK, BUT KEEPS GOING TO THE END."

1 Corinthians 13:4–7 MSG

When we arrived at the Golden Nugget, a local bar, "Wait for Love" by Luther Vandross, was playing. Linda and I decided earlier to go out to relax and catch up. We both were annoyed with the dating scene and needed an opportunity to express that frustration. We met at a local bar for a drink. I never indulged in alcohol. My dad drank enough beer for the whole world, and I decided as a child that I would never drink alcohol. While we were there, two good-looking men dressed to the hills came into the establishment and took note of us sitting together. Swiftly after the men's entrance, the barmaid approached our table with two fancy alcohol drinks. Linda and I told the giggling young lady that we had not ordered any drinks. The young lady then pointed to those two good-looking men seated at the bar, who wanted to say hello, via the drinks. I then asked the barmaid to thank the men and return my drink as I do not drink alcohol. However, as she was walking away from me and Linda, the two guys strolled over to our table to introduce themselves. Both gentlemen were very nice and respectful. Still caught in my feelings regarding "where are the good men?" conversation with Linda, I was not attentive to the gentlemen's conversation, and I decided to leave and go home. Linda and I always had a plan for our exit if we were together and one of us had a viable admirer. As I began to leave, Robert asked if he could walk me to my car. After a short conversation, he followed my vehicle to my house, and we sat in his car and talked until daylight. Four months later, we were married. As of the writing of this book, we have been married for thirty-six years.

Robert became my husband and life partner in September of that same year. On that night in May, I recall that Robert was a tall, self-assured man who worked at the General Motors Tonawanda Engine plant. He was kind and very secure in his skin. His perspective on life and dating was sexy and attractive. He was a hard worker. He was grateful for his job and the advantages it afforded him. He was raised in a neighborhood not far from my own. However, I was not familiar with his family. He is the oldest of five children who were raised with a father and a mother. I loved his parents. In my opinion, he had the best of both worlds: a doting mother and a dad who conveyed pride in his son as he ably followed in his dad's footsteps. I was thirty-one and Robert was thirty-five years old. Robert was very attentive. He respected my children and acknowledged their father. He did not take anything for granted. He always asked what my needs were. He demonstrated that he wanted to please me, and I wanted to please him. When we decided to get married, Marvin was delighted to share with his neighborhood friends that his mother was getting married. Ironically, one day one of his friends shared that his uncle was getting married on the same day as well. Both weddings happened on the same day at the same time with the same couple. Marvin found out that his mom was marrying his friend's uncle. Ain't God better than good!

Robert is my greatest supporter and biggest fan. I do not think there is anything that he believes I could not do with God's help. He was raised in a church very similar to the church I grew up in. His childhood memories of attending church were akin to mine. He followed in his father's footsteps and landed a job at General Motors. After we married, we talked often about where we have traveled and where we would like to travel. Loving Robert is easy. He held space for me to be real and to be the best mom I could. Robert cooked many dinners, grocery shopped, and looked after the children just as good, and sometimes better, than I did. He was truly a helpmate in every way. I began to get a little worried when the plant began requiring a lot of hours of overtime. I reminded my husband that I am his partner. He does not need to work crazy overtime hours to take care of the children and me. Robert clearly let me know that he would be the provider for this family.

Eight years after my divorce, I married this wonderful man who was mature and self-assured. He wasn't overconfident or arrogant but was very clear about the life he wanted. My soul always believed that I would find love and happiness again. I would talk frequently to my mom and God all about the kind of man I wanted in my life, and I asked the Lord to prepare me for the man God wanted for me. I am safe and secure with Robert having my heart forever!

FOUR

Teaching

"... IF IT IS SERVING, THEN SERVE; IF IT IS TEACHING, THEN TEACH."

Romans 12:7, New International Version (NIV)

W hen I explored working and going back to college to earn a degree in teaching, Robert was one hundred percent on board. He would work all evening, come home, and set things up for the children for the next morning. He stood in the gap with the management of the house and the children and loved and encouraged me all night. I earned a bachelor's degree in English in 1991, a Master of Science in Education in 1993, a permanent New York State teaching license, and secured a teaching position in August 1993 at Public School #66 (North Park Academy). My younger sister, Gwen, was my inspiration for getting into the teaching profession. She had been a teacher for many years, and I would harass her and her close colleagues about teaching. However, as I talked with Gwen over the years about her craft, I was impressed with the relationships she had with her students and their families. She cared deeply for them and her work. I was excited about teaching and my school placement. My assigned school was five minutes away from my home, and life was pretty good.

Two years into my first teaching job, I came down with the flu or pneumonia. I was very sick and directed to stay home by my physician. I was so concerned that my students would miss a lot of content and instruction and therefore get behind in school work. I continued designing creative lessons in my absence. I worked from my bedroom and took naps as needed. My husband purchased a fax machine to help me get the lesson plans and related documents to the substitute teacher more efficiently. This worked very well with the substitute teacher, and we were able to talk in the evening over the phone and make whatever adjustments were needed. After two weeks, I was released by the doctor to return to work. On the morning of my return, I was standing in the front office, checking in with the clerk, when my mentor teacher excitedly greeted me. She inquired about my health, and I told her I felt much better and was glad to be back at school. My mentor teacher appeared to be happy I was feeling better and able to return to work. She assured me that she checked on my students and everything went well with the substitute teacher in my absence. I was proud to let her know that the substitute teacher and I communicated nightly via telephone and my lesson plans and assignments were submitted via the office fax machine.

My mentor teacher shared her awareness of my procedures and seemed to look at me approvingly. However, she unexpectedly began goading me. I still hear her words clearly, "Oh, you are one of those uppity niggers, huh, having a fax machine." At that point, the world literally stopped! My stomach was queasy. My legs buckled under me, and I grabbed for the front counter in the office. The words kept repeating in my head. I wondered if I misheard what she said. I questioned myself if I really hear the N-word or if I added it to her declaration of me being uppity. In slow motion, I remembered circling around and looking at the clerk to figure out if anyone else heard that statement. Well, the people in the office indeed heard it and seemed to be frozen in place. My heart pounded in my ear. The sweat flowed from my hair and face. I was out of balance. I was angry and the tears welled up quickly. I wanted her to be held accountable. I immediately started to search in my mind for interactions and previous conversations we might have had that would indicate to her that the use of the N-word was appropriate. Then, almost as shocking as hearing the N-word, I realized that I was at school in the front office. I worked hard to keep my body calm, keeping my arms at my side and to not jump or move quickly. I felt powerless to act and powerful enough to hurt her. I demanded that she tell me why it was fitting to call me the N-word. She said it so effortlessly. My mentor teacher stared as if in shock and insisted she did not imply it in a derogatory way. She finished her rant by implying that I should know her better than that.

Seconds later, Principal Curtain entered the office upon learning what happened minutes before. He asked me to come to his office to calm down and talk. I was thinking, *Shit! Why do Black people always have to calm down and talk when racist white people pull this kind of shit?* I told him that I was not able to talk at that moment and requested to be left alone. He provided coverage for my classes while I struggled to gain my composure and figure out what to do. Before I left work for the day, the principal asked me for advice on how to resolve the matter. More insult to injury! The resolution should be to fire this teacher. He needed to declare to the staff that racist language will not be tolerated and that there is a stiff penalty for such actions. But no, he wanted me to relieve him of doing his job to appropriately deal with the racist actions of one of his white colleagues, or perhaps suggest some minimal consequence that would exonerate the white teacher. I was not about to make it easy for him or my mentor teacher.

By this time, the word had gotten out in the building about what had happened earlier that morning in the office. The word was out there that I was not going to let it go. The next day, the principal set up a meeting with the mentor teacher, me, and a district representative to mediate the incident and seek an amicable resolution. By this time, the building teachers, counselors, aides, and other staff had begun to choose sides along racial lines. The district sent a black female administrator to facilitate a civil conversation between the two of us separately. She met first with my mentor teacher and then with me. Nothing of significance was shared with me regarding the conversation with my mentor teacher. The facilitator encouraged me to be open to hearing the situation from another point of view. Whose point of view might that be? The administrator was a well-dressed older woman who spoke softly and with intention. She had many years of district-level administrative experiences in cultural competency work. The principal was confident in the administrator's ability to redirect my anger for a sufficient outcome to this situation.

The separate mediation sessions were expertly focused on shifting my anger to recognizing that I am wrong about my mentor teacher's intent using the offensive language. The facilitator resolutely stated that the mentor teacher did not use the N-word in the manner I believed she used it. Really? How many ways can a white person deliver the N-word to a black person with no intent to harm? Is there a menu of options? The mediation failed completely to come up with a viable resolution. This infuriated the principal and he decided that I was not trying to resolve the situation amicably. He transferred me out of his building. He claimed someone had to go, and the mentor teacher was tenured. He said the teacher's union would never support any decision to transfer her out. Principal Curtin was a remarkable participant in the confrontation. At times, he appeared to allow time and space during work hours for me to work through my position and figure out if I could move forward, but at the same time, I felt there was a real sense of urgency to get over my reaction quickly and neatly.

One day prior to leaving the building, he asked to speak with me. He informed me that he respected my work as a teacher and would like to keep me in his building. However, he wanted me to figure out a tangible way to make that happen. Well, I knew exactly what that meant. He wanted me to lay this thing to rest for the good of the order in the building, but really it was for his good. He did not want to deal with it. I listened to his self-serving and disingenuous ranting. He inquired regarding my background and future educational goals. Finally, I stopped him right there! Reading between his words, I realized that he was basically warning me that his approach would be better for me in the long run versus an involuntary transfer out of his building. At that point, I was mortified. I felt he was threatening my future endeavors if I do not comply to his terms. I could not hold back the tears or my disdain. I was so disgusted. I told the principal about what happened to my neighbor friend back in seventh grade at Public School #78 and how the local newspaper reported that busing desegregation was going well for the black children in the schools. That was an outright lie, but white people get to determine the impact of a situation and control the narrative. I was determined that was not going to happen with this matter. Principal Curtain suddenly became particularly interested in my seventh-grade story at Public School #78. He interrupted me a couple of times to ask me if I recalled any of my teachers' names. I did and I rattled a couple of names off to him. I told Mr. Curtain what really stuck with me was that white people never hold themselves accountable when they are wrong. In fact, white people support other white people regardless of the horrible infractions all the time. I ended by sharing my disgust for him as he is maintaining the same scenario in his building.

At this point, I knew my conversation was all over the place and I was rambling in agony, but then again, the seventh-grade incident resurfaced because the pain was identical at that moment. I did not plan to share that incident, but his demeanor opened the floodgates. Principal Curtain stopped me from continuing to inform me that he was the assistant principal at Public School #78 in the late '60s. Of course, he remembered the busing desegregation initiatives and the court rulings. His viewpoint was that the situation was a difficult time for everyone involved. Upon reflection, Principal Curtin talked about how the lack of preparation and planning by lawmakers and the school district produced great heartache for city residents in both neighborhoods. When I queried him concerning the oppressive encounters the black children suffered from passive-aggressive white teachers and administrators who intentionally tried to destroy our confidence and love for learning, he retreated in silence to undeniable dominance.

After that conversation, I was very comfortable moving on to a new school building. I did not believe it was my job to teach him and other white people the qualities of being humane, but, God! On the other side of the shared racial assault was the blessed opportunity to work with two marvelous Afrocentric, conscientious educators, Florence Rozier and Dolores (Dee-Dee) Bolden, who also worked at Public School #66. Florence was a school counselor and Dee-Dee worked in speech and hearing. They were well read on Afrocentricity and the history of black folk. They knew the work of several African scholars and were designing cross-grade-level lesson plans to support the academic work of all children, but especially black boys and girls. I was grateful to work with them and launch my own endeavors to study my history. As we continued to work together, we became friends and family members in every sense of the word.

FIVE

No Matter What You Face in Life, Do Not Let Go of God's Hand

> *"DAY AND NIGHT, I'LL STICK WITH GOD; I'VE GOT A GOOD THING GOING AND I'M NOT LETTING GO. I'M HAPPY FROM THE INSIDE OUT, AND FROM THE OUTSIDE IN, I'M FIRMLY FORMED."*
>
> Psalm 16:8–9 MSG

After my involuntary transfer from Public School #66, I resumed my career at Public School #11 on Floss Avenue in Buffalo. This was a kindergarten through eighth grade elementary school, located in the heart of an active drug-infested neighborhood. A colleague in the school district emailed an inquiry to me as to whom I might have upset downtown when she learned of my new placement. It was not a well-regarded school. The colossal word of warning came clearly through the email message. I replied to her concerns asking for an explanation for what she was implying. She informed me that Public School #11 was declared the worst school in the city! The colleague further implied I must have made somebody mad downtown. As far as I was concerned, Public School #66 was the worst teaching site in the city, so I took her words with a grain of salt.

I enjoyed working at Public School #11. There was a great team of caring teachers and staff. We talked frequently about the needs of our students and how we could meet them in our individual classes. The children came mostly from the neighborhood; very few students were bused there. The students responded well to patience and family like, take-no-excuses attitudes from the adults to encourage their best behavior and work. Over the years, adults who were children that attended Public School #11, upon their reflection, shared with me in supermarkets and upon running for a school board seat light posts of affirmation announcing to the world that I had made a difference in their lives. I am forever grateful to God for the light!

On Monday, December 8, 1997, at the age of seventy-five, my dad took his last breath at home, seated in his favorite recliner chair. My niece Kim lived upstairs, and I believed she discovered him there that morning. Dad had heart and blood pressure issues that he dealt with via prescription medications. Shortly after my mother's funeral, I took an opportunity to talk with my dad regarding the paternal pronouncement allegation hurled at me by an unfamiliar and unkind man. Not all my siblings were in favor of me addressing Dad about my paternal lineage. One sibling feared I might cause my dad to have a heart attack and die, given the nature of that conversation and Dad being emotionally fragile and still mourning. I believed she wanted to protect Dad versus blocking me from seeing answers. But then, other siblings encouraged me to do what I thought was best for me.

My maternal grandmother had not returned home to Washington, DC, yet when I sat with her to talk about Mommy. I felt great sorrow for my grandmother having to bury another child. Mama and Grandma looked physically similar and enjoyed many of the same activities in life. Both women loved to play cards for money, and both smoked cigarettes. I loved my grandma and grandpa very much. My grandpa, who I learned was my step-grandfather, had already passed some time before my mom did. They were great parents, and they doted on my mom. She was their oldest child and dedicated to the family members. She visited D.C. and Hampton often and helped them whenever she could.

Finally, I worked up the nerve to ask my grandmother if she knew anything about dad not being my biological father and if she knew another man was claiming he was my father. My grandma remained solemn and quiet for a while. Her daughter was her rock. She glanced at me with trepidation and replied that she really did not know if any of that was true. Her beautiful brown hands were motionless. It was revealed that Mom did confide in Grandma, when she was carrying me, that my dad may not be the father. Grandma told me that mom was incredibly disappointed in herself and did not want to break up her family. She encouraged Mom to talk with her husband and make it right. My grandmother then stretched out her short arms, and we hugged. She shook her head in rhythm. I embraced her and she would not easily let me go. We cried. I apologized for bringing this mess to her at this time. She was very attentive to my concerns and encouraged me to do whatever I believed I needed to do. Grandma supported my decision to approach my dad. Very calm and stately while speaking, she hinted that Dad will not be shocked with my questions and it was all going to be OK. I asked my grandma did she know how my mom and dad worked it out. She responded that mama never really talked about that situation again.

When I visited Dad, I was filled with guilt for interfering with his grieving with my self-centered need to have answers immediately. Dad was an encourager and believed in me. He would tell me to reach for the moon, and when you reach for the moon, you will surely land on the stars. A part of me wanted to walk away from the absurdity of questioning his fatherhood right then and there. I could have walked away but I did not. I was trying to reconcile my feelings from the past, getting kicked out of the house while pregnant. Was that the line in the sand for my dad? After all, he poured a lot of life into somebody else's child. He taught her everything she needed to be a responsible adult, and teenage pregnancy was the outcome. I continued to wonder why my mother was so quiet when my dad kicked me out. Why didn't she fight to keep me in the house, fight for me?

Dad's grief-stricken eyes appeared vacant as he sat in his favorite recliner in the sitting room in front of the TV. I apologized for bothering him and asked if there was anything I could get him, perhaps something to eat. He responded that he did not want anything. I asked if he pleased with Mom's homegoing service. He said he was. I knew there was nothing more to say to ease the incredible pain of losing a wife of thirty-five years. I continued on to inform him that a stranger at the funeral said something crazy to me, and I needed to talk to him about it. My voice was cracking, and my palms were sweating. Dad did not talk often about serious things during the period of Mom's illness. While Mama was sick, I tried many times to engage him in a conversation about his feelings regarding her cancer. He rejected any logic that he needed to talk about it. Some days, his pain paralyzed him, and he was not willing to help with her care. He would just sit quietly in the room while his children took care of everything. He was a proud man in control of his provision for his wife, but cancer does not allow anyone to control it or its circumstances. He was angry that he could not make things better for my mom and that she was, in fact, going to die soon.

Dad began sharing with me stories about his and Mom's relationship. He told me about a period they were disconnected and foolishly allowed people to hold emotional space in their union. Some things people said were true, and some were not. Drinking and jealousy was certainly a part of the interruption. Mom shared with Dad her concerns regarding the pregnancy with me. After the discussion, Dad believed there was an equal chance that the pregnancy was within the marriage as well as it was not. I was surprised by his words. They seemed consequently matter of fact and empty. I was not sure, at that moment, what to do with my perspective. I was perplexed and sad. Dad went on to say that their decision was to raise this baby, me, alongside the other children in the family. I asked him to share what he thought today regarding paternity. He believed I am his biological daughter.

In 2000, I left Public School #11 to teach in a high school. My cherished sista-friend Florence and I agreed to apply to a doctoral program at the State University of New York at Buffalo (UB). We befriended some of the great Black scholars of African history (Dr. Mwalimu Shujaa; Dr. Asa Hilliard III; Dr. Kofi Lomotey; and Dr. Henry Durand, to name a few), and they were happy to guide us through successful completion of the Doctor of Philosophy degree. At the time, New York State Assemblyman Arthur O. Eve Sr. was sponsoring a scholarship grant for black graduate students, who were interested in a post master's degree program. I applied and was conferred the Schomburg Fellowship Scholarship Award for my high score on the GRE. This scholarship funded my entire doctoral degree tuition, my books, and a stipend. There were many challenging nights and long telephone conversations with Florence over many cups of coffee. That was the only time in life I drank coffee. It was an intense program of study, and I was overjoyed taking this journey with Florence. We both had children in school, were working full-time, and studying as well.

A couple of years before Florence and I set our sights on this journey in higher learning, my husband's son Robert came to live with us. This was not a planned occasion. However, this eighteen-year-old young man shared that he decided during high school that he would go to Buffalo and live with his father after graduation. Robert grew up in Tennessee with his mother and two brothers, Chad and Tony. He loved his brothers, and over time I loved them as well. My girlfriends were concerned about the challenges that may come with another teenager in a very small house. Well, our house was disrupted in a big and beautiful way, one that I could not have imagined in million years. He looked like his dad and displayed his mannerisms. Robert and my children got along well. When he arrived, we were living in a small three-plus bedroom house with one bathroom. It was tight, but the boys were able to make use of the basement area for space to hang out and sleep sometimes. The neighborhood we lived in had flooding issues that often permeated the floors of the basement. The boys would descend on the basement like a wrecking crew to suction the water out of the basement. My son Robert found a job relatively easily at a retail store. He would let me know when new women's clothing arrived at the store. He was the oldest child of the clan and often would beat his siblings and Dad with birthday and Mother's Day gifts for me. Of course, he was a beloved in the Tigg family as the first grandchild, and he spent many summers here in Buffalo with his Granny, but he was a gem in my life. Along with his dad, Robert offered one hundred percent support while I worked on my PhD. He would make late night runs to the store to get me snacks, coffee, or something sweet. Sometimes, he would sit and listen as I read sections of an article or passages from my writing.

One incredibly sad day, after Robert had moved to Hagerstown, Maryland, for work, his brother Tony called to inform us that Robert was very ill and hospitalized with pneumonia. My husband and I were very worried. A couple of times we talked to Robert for short conversations. He said he was feeling better each day. I think that is something our children automatically say to their parents, but probably on many instances it is not the truth when it is said. After about a week, he was still hospitalized and seemingly not getting better. My husband and I left the following morning. We arrived and Robert was very weak and sick. He could barely talk or breathe. We took turns sitting with him and telling him how much we loved him. He would nod in affirmation. On January 28, 2018, our son

Robert passed way. All the kids loved each other tremendously! The grief was intense, and we continue to miss him daily.

Robert and I connected far beyond any level of love I could ever imagine in my finite mind. This very kind young man reminded me of the TV character Gomer Pyle from *The Andy Griffith Show* from the late '60s. Like the TV character, Robert was naïve and gentle. He would ask many questions about his father. He wanted to know his dad better. He loved his mother tremendously and shared the challenges he faced growing up without his dad. Robert encouraged me to be concerned about the impact of divorce placed on my children. I think the absence of their dad in the house was the kind of experience that connected all our children. This young man was easy to live with. He was considerate and respectful of anything I asked of him. I was happy to help him with applying and securing jobs. He had the work ethic of his dad. He never had to be pushed to go to work. He was determined to be responsible and accountable. Robert C. Fugate was our special gift from God!

The academic work in the doctorate program was voluminous and intense. Florence and I enrolled in the Educational Leadership and Policy program at UB. We had great black advisors and faculty who willingly took the role as supporter and encourager during our college experiences. Professor and Dissertation Committee Chair Dr. Henry Durand was genuine in his guidance and grandfatherly in his approach. He taught statistics and was very confident in his instruction and student outcomes. He assured students that he was an expert, and if they showed up and did the work, they would pass his course with flying colors. It took a little more than colossal instructor confidence for Florence and me to succeed in college-level statistics, so, Dr. Durand cheerfully made time afterhours at Burger King on Main and Bailey streets for Florence and me to receive extra help.

In 2001, Florence and I travelled to Ghana, West Africa, with Drs. Lomotey and Shujaa, advisors and committee members for our doctoral work. It was a phenomenal trip physically and emotionally. We went home to the Motherland! We visited Accra, Kumasi, Cape Coast, and Agona Duakwa. The warm embrace and welcome back home by the Ghanaian people were terrific. Upon leaving the plane, we quickly noticed the heat and all the beautiful colors displayed on clothing, buildings, and everywhere. There was a distinct sweet and woody fragrance like sandalwood incense. On August 2, 2001, our group received Ghanaian names at an Akan (renaming ceremony) at Agona Duakwa. This was a formal occasion where the Ghanaian community came together with ritual and dance to celebrate the new name given. My Ghanaian name is Ama Serwaa-Akoto. Ama means Saturday born, Serwaa means a beautiful present from God (the beautiful one), and Akoto is my family name. Florence was named AFua Gyesiwah, which means born on a Friday and has the fighting spirit. Next to marrying my husband and the blessing of sharing life with four children, the naming ceremony was the greatest experience of my life.

After thirty-five years of smoking cigarettes, with the help of the Lord, I quit smoking in Accra, Ghana. I was the only person in our education tour group who smoked cigarettes. I purchased a carton before I left for the motherland. At night, Florence would grudgingly go with me outside the hotel while I smoked. The dark in Ghana was extremely dark; no light was visible for miles. You could not see your hand in front of you. After about the second time escorting me outside to smoke, Florence informed me that she would not continue to go outside in the blackest of night with lots of creepy sounds to be with me while I smoked. She decided it was time that I should quit smoking.

The next day I quit cold turkey! In 2005, Florence and I earned our doctoral degrees. It felt fantastic to be called doctor and to embrace such a high level of achievement. I felt my parents' presence throughout the course work, cheering me on, and it was crucial that I embody and honor them by hyphenating my marital name with my birth name with the doctor prefix. Dr. Theresa A. Harris-Tigg.

While teaching at Public School #11, I met a very creative home education teacher named Rose Swift McKeller, who was in the process of building a new house in the Walden Heights development on the east side of Buffalo. This development included beautiful large single-family homes. We became friends very quickly, as I was in awe at her sewing and craft skills. I would tag along with her every lunch period to visit the area off Walden where her new house was being built. It was fascinating watching her house come to fruition. Over dinner, I would repeatedly tell my husband all about Rose's house. I would keep my eyes on the new housing developments in Buffalo. In 2005, Robert and I purchased our home in that development. I enjoy living there. I see my former students often when we shop in the neighborhood. My students behave differently when they see me in the supermarket versus in the school cafeteria. Sometimes, they are timid and other times ecstatic with the familiarity. When I campaigned for the city school board, many of my Public School #11 students made themselves and their support known to me. There is a greater acclaim for an educator when they touch the lives of young people.

Karla, Arius (grandchild #2), and great-grandchild #5 ultrasound image

Armon, Tiarra, and A'leia - great-grandchild #4

Brooklyn and Izeal IV - grandchildren 6 and 8

Xaiver, grandchild #1

Dad, me, and siblings

Mom and Dad wedding pic

Debbie, Gwen, and me

Dolores and Ashley

Dr. Theresa A.Harris-Tigg and Dr. Florence Flakes-Rozier

Izeal IV - grandchild #8 and Javon - grandchild #7

High School picture

Hubby and Me

Izeal III and Ebony

Jason and grandchildren

Jason, Jayden, and Dante - grandchildren 10, 11, and 9

Jason

Javon - grandchildren seven

Javon and Jason

Jaylen, grandchild #3 with great-grandchild Jaliyah #1

Jayliyah and Jaylen – great-grandchildren one and three

Jayliyah and us

Jazmin - grandchild number 5

Justice

King Ezra – great-grandchild two

Marvin and Ronda

Marvin, Armon, and Arius

Me teaching at McKinley H.S.

Me

Mom and me

Me

Sharon Jones, Hubby, Deborah Cooper, and Linda Preston

Robert C. Fugate, son

Robert and Theresa

Shelia B, Author's Academy, and me

The lineage – Grandma Earline, Mama, me, and Ebony

Theresa and siblings

Us

Me and hubby / Papa and Nana

SIX

Losing a Sibling

I was shocked and terrified around 2005, when my oldest sister Dolores told me she was very sick. By this time, we bonded as grown women as well as sisters. I was no longer *just* her sister. We talked on the phone every night before going to bed, into the early hours of the morning. We would talk about anything, everything, and everybody. I was grateful for our relationship because she was always so supportive of me, except when I divorced my first husband. She had grown very fond of him. Both of us were her protégés, and she had invested a lot of time and energy to helping us to mature and survive marriage. When I decided to end the marriage, my sister believed I had not weighed the decision carefully. I refused to recant. Unbeknownst to my family, I prayed and prayed about the decision, but once it was made, I was sure it was the best thing for me, so I stood my ground and proceeded with the legalities until the divorce was concluded. Initially, our relationship was severely impacted by my decision, and my sister wouldn't talk to me for many months.

By two years or so after the divorce, Dolores and I were long past rehashing my marriage misfortune. She and I reconnected and began talking to each other late at night again. I would listen for hours about her travel adventures with her best friends. They were called the "golden girls."

My sister enjoyed traveling to Las Vegas and other places. She would shop for days to have just the right outfits to walk around the casino. We would talk about how Robert and I were doing in the second marriage. She said the moment she met Robert she knew he was perfect for me. She liked him a lot. Robert absolutely loved Dolores. We would also talk about her job as an OR technician and working with doctors and nurses. She had great stories to share about how close her friends at work had become.

Dolores had been my idol since I was a little girl. I imitated her singing and dancing with her friends. I admired her loyal friendships with guys and girls from high school. They were dedicated to each other and watched each other's back. Some of her boyfriends were a little crazy, but others were the nicest people you could ever meet. All marriages have trying periods that can be emotionally draining. Her marriage was no different. She talked about things women should do to cope with stress at work and home. When she called to tell me that she was sick, I was shocked and not prepared! I listened as best I could, while at the same time I experienced paralysis in my limbs. I could not fathom my sister having cancer. Almost as stunning, Dolores decided at that point in her life to live on her own and get an apartment. I was all in, no matter what the challenge would be or how long it would take for my sister to be at peace. She was ecstatic in her new apartment. She loved decorating and designing beautiful spaces; she had a talent for that. Everything had a place and was in its place. Her contradictory circumstance of life was difficult at her age. Clearly, a new energy for life was blossoming, a new mature independence, while at the same time her body was being eaten away by cancer. I laughed a lot with Dolores during this time, and I cried a lot at home in the arms of Robert.

My sister Dolores died in 2006 from cancer that metastasized to her lungs. It is very tough to experience the death of a sibling. You do not expect it. My sister taught me so much. Our parents told the story how my oldest sister had to take her four siblings everywhere she went. She was the resident babysitter. Dolores tried to convince her friends that her siblings were bad children, but her friends told me later that she secretly liked taking us around with her. As a teenager, I remember many of the boyfriends or suitors (the guys interested in dating my sister). Because my sister had to watch us all the time, the guys would come to the house with treats and scary stories to get us to go to sleep early in the evening so they could visit and talk. My sister and I talked a lot about her three children. I was ecstatic, and I believed she had them just for me. She had two boys and one girl in the middle. My sister worked as an OR technician for years at local hospitals. Back then, they trained you on the job. At one point they decided to stop training on the job at the hospital and moved the program to a two-year college. Because it was the last class at the hospital where my sister worked, she thought this career would be great for me and the timing would be perfect. She wanted me to apply for the job. I refused. I had experience working in the hospital, but I was not interested in cleaning up blood or seeing people knocked out. She was a little disappointed because she wanted someone she knew to have this opportunity. We put our heads together to brainstorm who would be suitable to get this good moneymaking job. We finished each other's sentence when we determined it to be her daughter, Kim! My niece would be the perfect candidate— at least we thought so. Kim agreed to our coercion and completed the training, secured the job, worked at the local hospital with her mother until her death, and continues to this very day there.

SEVEN

The PhD Life

In August 2006, I accepted a position as assistant professor at a higher learning institution in the city. I taught English education courses in preparation for college students to become secondary classroom English teachers. For the most part, I taught white females. The number of white males was growing, however. We had minimal numbers of black males and females. When I started at the college, the department was facing a reaccreditation process. I was appointed coordinator of the secondary English education program to ensure the accreditation reports were completed and submitted in a timely fashion. The department's culture established a clear split between the English and the education faculty. The English faculty taught literature and humanity courses. The education faculty taught method courses and pedagogy. Most of the full-time English and education faculty were white. I was the only full-time, tenure track African American faculty during my time there. In 2010, I was granted tenure but denied promotion. One male English faculty fought intensely to convince the white personnel committee that my research work was not scholarly enough. My research focused on culturally responsive teaching and learning of African American students. Later, there were attacks made on my character. One staff person, a white female, concocted a story about an altercation I supposedly had with a school principal. Despite the fact the school principal refuted any such altercation ever happened, this untruthful narrative was proclaimed to be true because the chair valued the storyteller. I used to say you cannot make this stuff up, but in a racist system, they can!

In 2010, two colleagues and I travelled to South Africa. It was the dream of a lifetime. We visited several schools in Soweto, a township of the city of Johannesburg, and the Cape of Good Hope. The children in Soweto wore uniforms to school. They were very excited to see the delegation from the United States. In addition, we visited Oprah Winfrey's fifty-two-acre, all-girl's academy campus. It is a boarding school for girls grades eight through twelve, located in Gauteng Province, South Africa. The academy was beautifully designed with cutting edge technology and a strong support network for the girls to succeed in all areas of life. Lastly, we visited the house where President Nelson Mandela lived in South Africa and saw Shanti villages. These villages consist of poor buildings and living spaces typically made with mud, tarps, and wood. The humble homes were placed very close together. The infrastructure of safe water and electricity was challenging for its residents.

In 2013, a seat on the Buffalo School Board became available, and the board was seeking applications for those interested. Each seat on the board represents an educational district in the city. I lived in the East District. After careful consideration, I decided to apply for the position. After application submission, I was called for an interview. I thought I did well in the interview but shortly thereafter, I learned that the board selected someone else. The seat was designated as an appointment, because the former board member left the seat before the end of the term. When the appointment was made public, several residents in my district encouraged me to consider running for the seat when the term ends, so I did! I ran for the seat, won the majority votes of my constituents, and won the seat again for the second term. I served the board from 2013–2019. The Board of Education is comprised of nine members and one employee, the superintendent.

My experience as a board member was very interesting. I was nominated and elected by board colleagues to the position of Vice President of Student Achievement. I held that title for both terms. Every board member has schools in their district that are monitored for academic achievement, health and safety, disciplinary data, and attendance (students and staff). I had a total of nine schools in the East District. I visited the schools at least once per month, more if there were special programs or events happening at a school. In addition to visiting schools, members were encouraged to build a relationship with parents and community members. I attended parent-teacher organization meetings and represented the East District at city and statewide events. As VP of Student Achievement, I had to be aware of the teaching and learning resources in all the schools. That is about fifty to sixty schools. There were weekly meetings every Wednesday that lasted for approximately six to seven hours and sometimes longer. During my tenure, board members were able to remove a member who frequently used racist language during meetings and who shared confidential information with the public. This entailed court proceedings and travels to Albany, New York, to testify. I enjoyed the board work. Many times, the conversations at the board table were contentious and difficult. The board is made up of diverse people from all walks of life. There is no prerequisite of education or experiences to be a board member, nor do you need a working knowledge of the educational policies or practices. However, you must live in the city of and not be a current employee of the district. In addition to visiting schools, I had to read pages and pages of voluminous documents. I had to verify data and attend meetings to analyze data and learn about the school officials' interpretations and reports.

On March 16, 2014, I was ordained a deacon at my current church under the tutelage of my Pastor Jacquelyn Ross Brown. I was called by God to serve as a deacon many years before; however, there was no official ordination process a long time ago. The ordination training included daily personal prayer, group prayer, spiritual meditation, biblically based training/instruction, a public review, and successful completion of a test. Shortly thereafter, I was nominated and elected to serve as the chairwoman of the diaconate ministry. God has been so good to me all my life, and the call to serve was eagerly accepted.

In 2019, I had to endure a very personally challenging year. I mourned the loss of four beautiful spirits, whom I had the blessing of knowing, loving, and calling friends in the physical realm on earth. It is in our tradition as African people to always continue to call the names of our beloved loved ones who have gone to live with the Lord. The African proverb says that if you call their name, they will never die. So, with a full heart I say the names of my sista-friends Debra Sevillian-Poles, Gail Lucas, Dr. Florence Flakes-Rozier aka Afua Geysiwa, and Angela Yevette Croxie. Ase'.

EIGHT
Wealth and Unspeakable Joy!

"I HAVE BEEN HONORED AND BLESSED WITH MANY YEARS OF COMPLETE JOY LOVING AND RAISING MY CHILDREN (ROBERT, MARVIN, EBONY, AND JASON). I HAVE THEIR ACCOMPLISHMENTS, HURTS, PAIN, AND STRUGGLES ENGRAVED IN MY HEART FOREVER, AND THAT IS THE GIFT THAT COMES FROM LOVING AND SHARING IN THE GROWTH OF OUR FAMILY. I'VE FOUND MY PEACE, AND I'VE MADE IT THROUGH."

—Mom

"IF I HAD A STAR FOR EVERY REASON FOR WHY I LOVE MY GRAND/ GREAT GRANDCHILDREN, I WOULD HAVE THE WHOLE NIGHT SKY."

—Author unknown/Nana

In late fall of 1994, November 3rd, I nervously stood next to Ebony's side, as she had spent several hours in labor. This little boy was taking his time, and his mom was quickly starting to show signs of physical exhaustion as well as growing deep concern for how long it was taking for this little boy to make his arrival. While I stood in the labor and delivery room, in mask and gown, watching my baby girl working so very hard to do all she could to bring forth this wonderful gift from God; Lord, I gave you all the praise. Of course, I began to recall how she fought to arrive here on the planet when all the medical personnel told me she was gone. I thought about her kindergarten graduation, piano lessons, cheerleading, and confirmation classes. I cried as I felt so thrilled to be there with Ebony. This little boy weighed in at almost 9 lbs. He cried, and I cried at the sight of this infant king and all his grandness. I watched while the nurse swaddled him and gently and sweetly looked in his eyes. Yes, his eyes were wide open. The nurse then walked over to the side of bed where my daughter was receiving supportive medical attention. After a minute, she handed this beautiful bundle of joy to his dad. My heart was beating rapidly and loudly. Then, I was able to hold him. I held many babies in my time, but Lord, this little chocolate boy took my breath away. My heart began to slow down, and it was as if this little boy and I were breathing in sync with each other. He was so comfortable, and he just stared at me quietly and peacefully. The parents named him Xaiver Kaylen Riley. We call him Zay. Ebony and Zay lived with us for a while before his parents tied the knot in marriage. Zay came home to a pink and beige nursery room. Ebony was told she was having a girl right up until his birth. Well, it was such joy having him live with us, because I got to snuggle and love on him every day!

Thirty days after Zay's arrival, Marvin called to share the marvelous news that my second grandson had arrived, and Ronda, Marvin's wife, was doing well in labor and delivery at Sisters Hospital. This was December 3, 1994. Robert and I immediately got in the car and drove over to the hospital. Upon entering the hospital, I remember telling my husband that I needed to sit down one minute before getting on the elevator. My heart was racing, and I was overcome with deep thanks for all God has done in my live. I needed to be still for a moment; my first born having his first born! When I entered the hospital room, Marvin was practically in the bed with Ronda, and I could see from the door this little bundle had captured their attention. Oh my God, this little boy was glowing. He had dark colored eyes that just pierced through to your heart. Ronda looked beautiful, and Marvin had a big smile fixed on his face. You could feel the blessing in the room. When I held this little baby, the joy was tangible. I started to tear up, because he was as cute as a button. He weighed about three pounds more than his dad did at birth. (This little boy's dad was a preemie at birth and weighed 3 lbs., 2 oz.) He was named Arius Irving Prophet. I just loved holding Arius. He was a beautiful boy. Looking in those eyes, I knew he would be loving and funny! He had that look that said, *Just wait, I am going to keep you laughing, Nana.*

When the boys began walking, I purchased a kiddie swimming pool. Every warm Buffalo summer day, I would place that pool on the front lawn and fill it with water. The three of us—my two grandsons and me—would get in the pool and have a ball splashing each other. Robert and I had a decent sized backyard where we could enjoy the pool with the grandbabies. I subconsciously wanted to show them off and share my joy with the world! Arius is grown now with a beautiful wife, Karla, and on May 18, 2019, God blessed them with their first child, a son, Ezra. More about King Ezra later, when I add my great-grandbabies to the story.

Almost four years later, Armon arrived for his place in the Prophet-Tigg tribe! I call him Moni. His mom calls him Pooh-Bear. I clearly get it! Armon was born on May 30, 1998, in Fort Sill, Oklahoma, where his dad, Marvin, was stationed in the army. Shortly after the announcement, Robert and I boarded a plane for Oklahoma. When I first saw this baby boy, I instantly noticed his big, beautiful round face, juicy fat cheeks, and fat legs. He was very huggable and reserved. He just chilled in my arms and observed his surroundings. Armon and Arius loved to play basketball. Both boys were very skilled in basketball. I loved to watch them play. Both played in high school and Moni played in college. Wherever Marvin, Ronda, and those boys resided in the states or out of the country, Robert and I traveled there to visit. We loved our vacation to Germany. Armon is now all grown up and has a baby on its way (due 2022).

About six to seven weeks after the birth of Moni in 1998, on July 15th, my youngest son, Jason, had his first baby. He was called Jaylen Donald. We call him Jay for short. Something special happens inside of you when your baby has a baby! Young Jaylen had an energetic spirit. He was always ready to go do something. It was absolutely breathtaking watching this little boy play and grow. His physical movements were agile and flexible and beyond his years with a basketball. Both my sons enjoyed playing basketball, and I knew their sons would follow suit, but Jaylen was exceptional in basketball at an incredibly young age. My husband and I would go all over Buffalo to gym after gym seeing him play. Jay participated for years in the Gus Macker, a 3-on-3 basketball tournament in the city. After Gus Macker, I watched Jay playing basketball and observed his swift improvements. Jay and Moni shared the love of basketball as cousins and best friends. I enjoyed the many opportunities observing Jason as he watched and cared for Jay. The love this dad and son shared as he was growing was nothing short of spiritual. As of the writing of this book, Jay has two children of his own: Jayliyah (J.J.) and Jaylen (JuJu).

Then arrived my first granddaughter, Jazzy Mazzy, on September 14, 2003. Jazmin Isabella was a huge, bright light of hope and treasured love. She was a beautiful, fair-skinned baby inside and out! I was so excited to have a granddaughter. On her birthday, I shouted and praised the Lord throughout my house. She was a quick-moving little baby. I had so much fun playing with her and taking her to work with me. When she was five or so, I would take her to work at the college. She would sit on the floor in my office and turn the pages of books, invent words while she read to me. If I happened to be working on something and not given her storytelling the attention she wanted, she would wiggle her body between my desk and chair to get my attention. She was so funny! As she continued to grow, I could see the seeds planted for a real daddy's girl. It made my heart happy, glad to observe the love Jason has for his children. Jazzy has continued to inspire me with her intrinsic intelligence and prowess for basketball. I am so glad God saw to it that I can be here to witness my granddaughter's love of learning, playing basketball with such grace and skill, and walking boldly in her skin.

Brookie-Rookie is the nickname I call my second granddaughter. Her father Izeal and Ebony named her Brooklyn Theresa Joyce; she was born on June 23, 2005. At birth, she resembled Ebony exactly as she had looked at birth. She had the same beautiful features: a beautiful chocolate brown chip with a head full of coiled and curly hair. I was ecstatic about the birth of a second granddaughter. Brookie's eyes were always wide opened. She noticed things and would make funny faces. I didn't think it was just gas either. She observed her settings and responded emotionally with smiles or tears. The delivery with this little girl was much calmer than that for her older brother Zay. I looked forward to dressing her and picking out girly wardrobe items. However, the makings of an athlete were already showing. Well, she didn't have much choice—her dad is a track and field coach. As she began to grow into a little girl, Brookie would join me at work at the college with her cousin Jazzy Mazzy. Admittedly, I was clearly delighted to show off my girls at work. In high school, both girls became scholar-athletes. To God be the glory.

The year 2006 was filled with great joy. On March 5th, Jason's third child and my seventh grandchild was born. It was an instant bond. He has the eyes of his mother. He was a big loveable baby. Javon Donald was a kindhearted little boy who wore his heart on his sleeve. I call him JP. He adored following his dad around the house. He would think nothing in public to climb up on his dad's neck. You could see the bond they shared was strong. Robert and I spent a lot of time with Javon because he loved to hang out with his Nana and Papa. JP, like his father, uncle, big brother, and sister, loves to play basketball. In many ways, his basketball skills came upon him like it did for his big brother: quick and progressively. Watching JP play basketball was an art form activity; simply amazing. In school, JP kept good grades and a close relationship with his grandparents. We are grateful for his kind soul and spirit.

On May 25, 2007, another chocolate chip, as their mother calls them, graced this earth. Ebony and Izeal named him Izeal IV. He was a handsome baby boy with what my grandmother used to call "a good grade of hair." His hair was thick, curly, and manageable. His nickname was Izzy when he was little. I loved to watch Izzy dance and entertain his family, and I don't mean he would jump around and the adults called it a dance. This little boy danced like he had training. I never understood where his dance ability came from, but he was good at it. We would howl and make deep belly laughing sounds at his moves and dance configurations. Sometime around fifth or sixth grade, Izeal IV announced he did not want to be called Izzy anymore and that was the end of that. I enjoy Izeal's spirit and quietness. He is a great student who is intentional with learning.

Jason completes my grandchildren tribe with three more boys, numbers nine, ten, and eleven. Yes, your count is correct! Jason has six children: five boys and one girl. On October 19, 2008, Jason (grandson) was born. He was a very calm and sweet baby. He had very dark hair and eyes, a nice mixture of his mom and dad. I call him JJ. JJ has been a serious little boy. He is aware of what goes on around him and makes decisions quickly if he wants to participate in a specific activity. I can count on JJ to not be the child initiating horseplay in the house. He is more reserved than that. He always demonstrates great manners and consideration of others. I love being in his company, because he has great character. JJ also does very well in school. He plays a little basketball, but I think he prefers track and football.

Later came Dante Joseph, on October 19, 2009—the first of Jason's children whose name does not begin with the letter "J." He was a gorgeous little boy with generous eyes. He reminded me a lot of his dad when he was a baby, because both were so small and squirmy. Dante and his dad were fun to watch together. I think they have the same spirit, loving and playful. He is a multi-talented young man with good grades and behaviors in school. From some of his mom's Facebook posts, I believe Dante loves to dance as well. He plays baseball, basketball, and football. Dante lives in Niagara County, so I don't go to many of his games, but I hear about his improvements and touchdowns. He is always respectful and willing to help his grandparents with anything when he visits.

Lastly, and certainly not the least, is Jayden, who arrived on July 12, 2010. Looking a lot like his brother JJ, Jayden is filled with curiosity and wonder. He wants to know and try everything. Jayden was born with confidence in everything; there are very few things he will not try. I love his spirit. This little guy is so much fun to be around. He is adventurous and brave. He is not shy about taking the lead with his older brothers. Seemingly, he likes to have fun in school, more so than being a studious kid. However, just like all his siblings, he is very intelligent. He is the smallest and the youngest of his siblings, but he probably has the biggest heart for adventure. As a senior citizen, this is the child that encourages his grandparents to be ready for his visits because it will be an enthusiastic and fun-filled day.

I do not take the blessing of grandchildren for granted. There are truly no words available to describe how my heart feels about my eleven grandchildren. When they are happy, I am happy. When they hurt, I am hurting. It is a wonderful spiritual relationship that is forever. I will always love my babies. Now, as if God had not done enough to bless me with eleven grandchildren, our Lord's abundance of grace and mercy has allowed me live a life that involves great-grandchildren.

My first great-grandchild is a little girl named Jayliyah. We call her JJ. She was born on August 16, 2018. She carries the name of her father (Jaylen) and her mother (Quantia) to create the name Jayliyah. She is a wonderful little girl. I still have the video clip where, at nine months, she repeated after me the word "Nana." I am grateful to God that my grandson Jaylen thought it important for her to spend time with her great-grandparents. We have had the absolute pleasure of being with her almost weekly until the pandemic.

My second great-grandchild is Ezra. He was born on May 18, 2019. My grandson Arius and his wife Karla call him King Ezra, and I love that name. He is a very curious baby who is a nice blend of his mommy and daddy. His mother Karla is teaching Ezra her home language, Spanish. My daughter-in-love Ronda and Marvin are just overjoyed being with King Ezra, their first grandchild. I am not sure why they use the "King" before his name, but it is fitting. Ezra wraps everyone around his little finger. He is walking and trying to communicate some words. South Carolina will always be my home away from home if my King Ezra continues to live there. As of this writing, praise the Lord, Arius and Karla are expecting their second child.

Next came grandbaby Jaylen, who arrived on June 11, 2020. His parents call him Ju-Ju. Wow! He is the sweetest little boy in the whole world. He is truly a baby model. The facial expressions this little boy shows his confidence and determination. He wants to do all the things his big sister J.J. does right now. When they are over, he cries when I hold him until I put him on the floor so he can try to keep up with J.J. and our dog, Justice. The 2020 COVID-19 pandemic caused a big hole in my heart, as senior citizens were warned to be careful with the children. The World Health Organization and CDC explained that children could be super-spreaders of the deadly virus. Sadly, this serious situation limited our visitations from our great-grandchildren tremendously.

NINE

"Shelter in Place"

"MEANWHILE, THE MOMENT WE GET TIRED IN THE WAITING, GOD'S SPIRIT IS RIGHT ALONGSIDE HELPING US ALONG. IF WE DO NOT KNOW HOW OR WHAT TO PRAY, IT DOESN'T MATTER. HE DOES OUR PRAYING IN AND FOR US, MAKING PRAYER OUT OF OUR WORDLESS SIGHS, OUR ACHING GROANS. HE KNOWS US FAR BETTER THAN WE KNOW OURSELVES, KNOWS OUR PREGNANT CONDITION, AND KEEPS US PRESENT BEFORE GOD. THAT'S WHY WE CAN BE SO SURE THAT EVERY DETAIL IN OUR LIVES OF LOVE FOR GOD IS WORKED INTO SOMETHING GOOD."

Romans 8:28 MSG

I know this chapter seems out of place in a memoir, but that is exactly how this scary and deadly situation occurred: out of place and out of nowhere. The global health pandemic consisted of a deadly and infectious virus running rampant throughout the United States and the world. Our local officials would repeatedly warn citizens that if you don't have to go out, please stay home and shelter in place. We were required to wear a mask or facial covering and maintain six feet with social distancing from other people. The virus was determined to be airborne. There are so many things in life that are scary, but the joy of getting to know my great-grandbabies and then suddenly being not able to is disheartening. My thoughts were everywhere, and, in addition to that calamity, there was racial unrest emerging across the country. A lot of people died during this health and racial pandemic, as I named it. The clear message was to shut everything down. We could not attend worship service in church buildings.

Only essential businesses were open in the beginning of the pandemic in March. For the Thanksgiving holiday, we were directed by the CDC to have Thanksgiving dinner with only those people in your immediate household, with no open gatherings. In November of 2020, Joe Biden and Kamala Harris were elected president and vice-president, respectively. Vice President Kamala Harris is the first woman, and first woman of color, elected to office in the White House. Hope was on the rise again.

This forced quiet time at home afforded me the chance to look at all the things I am grateful for and to reevaluate what is important at this stage of my life. When I reflect on my life, as married senior citizen, grandmother, and great-grandmother serving the Lord as a deacon and doing educational consulting and college teaching, I am beyond grateful for my life. God has allowed a little black girl, a middle child fourth in line with her siblings, born on the eastside of Buffalo to two parents without a high school education, a child with a tiny little faith like a mustard seed, to grow and become fruitful, and where mountains of obstacles were moved out of the way. Now, this narrative is only a fraction of my life. I am writing this memoir so my grandchildren and great-grandchildren will have a sense of who I am and how good God is. My husband and I have been married thirty-five plus years. Both of us enjoy a reasonable portion of good health and an always-together-and-forever kind of rich, sustaining love.

When I look back and think about the goodness of the Lord, my heart is filled with joy and gratitude. I am happy for the life God graced me with. I have no regrets and would not want one event or circumstance to be changed one bit. I have had everything I needed and many of things and opportunities I desired. As I think about the world my grandchildren and great-grandchildren have inherited, I am often sad, because their lives are encouraged with a display on Facebook, Instagram, and other online platforms without discernment and taste. I want them to understand that this forever digital platform is unforgiving and never forgets. I want my grandchildren to know that each of them is capable of being great, because they can serve others. Our God inside of them is greater than the problems and stresses of the world. They can serve others and they can build a wonderful life for themselves with God's help. It takes just a little faith like that of a mustard seed, and our Lord and Savior will take care of each of them.

To all my grandchildren and great-grandchildren, I want you to know God and his miracles. You don't have to go to church; however, church is where encouragement, nourishment, and reassurance is plenty. The world is a tough place. There are many paths to navigate this earthly place filled with many opinions. The influencers start early in your lives, coercing your tastes in food, clothing, friendships, needs, and wants, but if you hold on to God's hand, through it all you will see that you are unconditionally loved and that you are the child of a King. God is better than good! God is a provider. God is a healer. God is a way-maker. God is your friend to the end. God is nearby. God loves you unconditionally. There is nothing you can do to fall out of God's love! God's grace and mercies are new and fresh each morning. You may turn from God, but God will never turn away from you. He is always forgiving. I am a witness to God's wonderful love and kindness through it all!

There were times in my life when I was at the end of my rope, when trouble surrounded me and I did not know what to do and where to go. I could not possibly tell all the stories in this one book. When I needed Jesus, all I had to do is call him and ask for help. Jesus has not failed me yet. Sometimes he quieted me while I waited. Sometimes, he protected me from things and forces I did not even know were trying to swallow me up. That is how good God is!

When I lost my mother, I was broken. I could not imagine my life without her. I did not know how to let go of her without falling apart. I thought my lungs would collapse. But God! The Lord came and quieted my breathing and my thinking. Peace came over me as God quieted my heart and assured me that I would always remember my mother and her love. I would always remember her smile and dancing, and I do. I can always feel her near me whenever I think about her. The "shelter in place" is Jesus Christ, our Lord and Savior. It is not frightening there. The Lord allows me, your nana, to dream about each of you, my beloved grandchildren, and how wonderful your life can be with Jesus. There will be times when you may feel alone. You may feel that no one understands you and that no one is even listening to you. I remember when I was a teenager how bothered I was by my parents' strict rules. We had to be in the house when the streetlights came on. In high school, I remember being mad that I could not go the places some of my friends could go. I felt they wanted us to be so different than other people; their standards were very high. Little did I know at the time, God's grace kept my attitude in check, so I was never disrespectful to them. I was not able to appreciate all my parents did and sacrificed at that time. God began showing me difficult things that other young people may age were going through and that could have just as well been me. I recalled my childhood religious teaching, and those memories strengthened me as grew into adulthood. Take care of yourselves. Be aware of what you are putting in your body and exposing your mind to. Always ask the question: Is this good for my body and soul or will it harm my body or soul? Your body is the temple where God resides, and you want to take good care of it. There is a cliché that says if you take care of your body when you are young, your body will take care of you when you get old. I believe I am living that saying.

Friendships are important, but real friends are few and far between. I have learned that you cannot be a friend to everyone. It really is life affirming to honor your mother and your father. Parents are not perfect. In fact, we all learned by trial and error along the way. I witnessed how much your parents loved each of you. Sometimes, plans do not work as we expect them to, and parents do not always stay together. I want to encourage you, my beloved grandchildren and great-grandchildren, to really see your parents as people doing the best they could at the time and see that their unfailing love for you is always right there. Remember to share with your parents your joys and struggles. Be patient if they are not immediately in agreement with your decisions. Listen to them without interrupting, and hear their heart. Both children and parents are gifts from God. Forever love your siblings and savor every minute you have together; have each other's back. As you get older and begin families yourselves, it often takes great effort to stay in touch with your brothers and sisters. It is worth the effort! Thank God for the opportunity the internet provides to stay in touch with pictures and updates of our family. Try not to get so wrapped in your own life that you isolate yourselves from your family. Believe in love! You are always enough! "Make every effort to add to your faith goodness; and to goodness, knowledge; and to knowledge, self-control; and to self-control, perseverance and godliness; and to godliness, brotherly kindness; and to brotherly kindness, love. For if you possess these qualities in increasing measure, they will keep you from being ineffective and unproductive in your knowledge of our Lord Jesus Christ" (2 Peter 1:5–8, NIV).

Finally, my life is so full of happiness, love, and adventure because of each of you. You bring unequivocal joy to my spirit. My sista-friends are the best on the planet! I am blessed with a huge circle of believers who continue to pray for me. My experiences are beyond what I thought I would ever encounter and accomplish. I really believe God always keeps angels all around me, and the rugged mountains of life surely did move! My goal for the rest of my days is to love and serve God and my neighbors better. Secondly, to encourage all grandmothers to write their story for their grandbabies.

Journey well, my loves!
Nana
Dr. Theresa A. Harris-Tigg, a.k.a. Ama Serwa Akoto